Wild Foods

Wild Foods

TEXT AND PHOTOGRAPHS BY
LAURENCE PRINGLE

ILLUSTRATIONS BY
PAUL BREEDEN

A beginner's guide to identifying, harvesting and cooking safe and tasty plants from the outdoors

FOUR WINDS PRESS   NEW YORK

*Dedicated to my favorites —
the wild strawberry and brown-eyed Susan*

Library of Congress Cataloging in Publication Data

Pringle, Laurence P
Wild foods
Bibliography: p.
Includes index.
Summary: A guide to identifying, collecting, and preparing
twenty wild plants commonly found in and
around fields, forests, and streams.
1. Cookery (Wild foods) — Juvenile literature.
2. Wild plants, Edible — Juvenile literature.
[1. Wild plants, Edible. 2. Cookery — Wild foods]
I. Breeden, Paul. II. Title.
ISBN 0-590-07511-X

Published by Four Winds Press
A division of Scholastic Magazines, Inc., New York, N.Y.
Text and photographs copyright © 1978 by Laurence Pringle
Illustrations copyright © 1978 by Scholastic Magazines, Inc.
All rights reserved
Printed in the United States of America
Library of Congress Catalog Card Number: 78-1910
1 2 3 4 5 82 81 80 79 78

Acknowledgments

The origins of some books can be traced to a specific year, date, and place. Not this one. Perhaps it began in the 1940s in upstate New York where I picked black raspberries, some for pies my mother baked, some for sale to earn precious pocket money. My family also dined on rabbit pot pie, venison, muskrat legs, and other game. The idea was planted: nature offers delicious wild foods.

For many years afterward, though, I was mostly a latent forager. Then, about 1970, I met Christopher Letts—naturalist, stone mason, shad fisherman, forager, and friend. For the first time I tasted sumacade and Japanese-knotweed pie. Writing an article about Chris led to more foraging, good eating, and to an extraordinary wild foods dinner on a day in May, 1976. One guest was editor David Reuther; we began talking about this book early in 1977.

I have tried to create a book that is especially helpful to a beginning forager and cook—which I was myself just a few years ago—and have received invaluable aid from editor David Reuther, copy editor Nancy Inglis, and designer Lucy Bitzer of Four Winds Press. To make identification as easy as possible, edible wild plants are shown in both photographs and Paul Breeden's detailed illustrations.

Chris Letts offered practical tips from his two decades of day-to-day foraging experience. Recipes were adapted from a variety of sources, but mostly from the books described in the Further Reading section. The practicality and variety of the recipes was enhanced by suggestions from my friend Lois Murphy, a teacher of gourmet cooking. Dr. Larry G. Pardue of the Horticultural Society of New York reviewed the manuscript for botanical accuracy. If any errors remain, they are mine.

Finally, a special warm thanks to Sean, Jeffrey, and Heidi Pringle, who posed for photographs and served as recipe-testers, and to Susan Klein, who enthusiastically shared the work and fun of foraging and cooking.

Laurence Pringle

201478

Contents

Wild Foods

Introduction

Not long ago, a person who ate dandelions and cattails was probably considered some kind of weird "nature nut." But not anymore. During the last few years there has been increasing concern about the quality of the food we eat. Many people believe that it is not healthy for humans to eat the heavily processed and artificially colored and preserved foods sold in supermarkets. As a result, many so-called natural foods—from wheat germ to yogurt—are growing in popularity. Inevitably, an interest in natural foods has led to the most natural foods of all—wild foods.

There are many benefits to foraging for wild foods. Those of us who live in cities and suburbs tend to forget how dependent we are on the soil, water, air, and sunlight. For many of us, it must seem that our food actually comes from the supermarkets themselves! Foraging helps dispel this notion. For a little while at least, we can be directly connected to nature; we can feel more in touch with the earth upon which we all depend. This may be the greatest benefit of foraging for wild foods.

This book is an introduction to the world of edible wild foods. Most of the plants included in this volume are available throughout the United States. They are all easily recognized and all are safe and delicious to eat. This book is also an invitation to join in the fun of finding, preparing, and eating wild foods. Chances are you will discover new tastes that you will enjoy for many years to come.

This roadside tangle of "weeds" is mostly edible plants: wineberry, black raspberry, milkweed, and lamb's-quarters.

Wild Foods, Naturally

For most of us, foraging for wild foods is a pleasant pastime; few people today need to depend on foods they find themselves. Yet at one time people ate only wild foods, obtaining all of their sustenance from hunting and fishing and the gathering of nuts, berries, roots, and other plant foods. Once they learned how to cultivate crops, they had more dependable food supplies and were thus able to stay in one area for long periods.

North American Indians ate mostly wild foods, although some tribes also cultivated such plants as corn (maize). Of course the origins of corn, like those of all of today's grains, vegetables, and fruits, can be traced back to wild plants.

The Europeans who first invaded North America also had to rely on the wild bounty of the continent they had "discovered." Sometimes explorers and settlers had to depend on killing wild animals and harvesting the seeds, fruits, nuts, and leaves of wild plants for their very survival. The Indians pointed out the edible species, sparing the newcomers the risks of trial and error.

This hunter-gatherer lifestyle has not yet vanished completely. Even today, some Australian aborigines and African Pygmies obtain much of their food from the wild.

Some descendants of European immigrants also carry on a tradition of foraging for wild foods. City-bound for most of the year, these people occasionally travel into the countryside in search of some of the same kinds of foods their ancestors ate. In many cases they may find the same species that grew in the "old country." Such edible plants as dandelion, plantain, and chicory were brought to North America from Europe. For these people, finding and eating wild foods is part of a tradition that has been handed down from generation to generation. This was true of the late Euell Gibbons, who was and still is the world's best-known forager. As a boy growing up in the Southwest, he was introduced to wild foods by his mother and his grandmother.

For some people, the outdoors is still a natural supermarket of tasty and nutritious foods. Without hesitation they plunge into fields, vacant lots, woods, or roadside tangles of vegetation and begin collecting berries, leaves, and other plant parts. They urge others to try the pleasures of foraging and tend to scoff at the dangers of poisonous plants. It is easy, they say, to find and identify the safe, edible ones. Everything they say is true—*for them*. It is not necessarily true for others. Many of us are far removed from our hunting-gathering ancestors. Just as some people come from a foraging tradition, others come from a city-dwelling, supermarket tradition. We may recognize only a few kinds of wild plants—mostly the weeds we seek to banish from our lawns.

For many people, nature is thus not a natural supermarket but a bewildering mass of greenery. It may look nice, but it is rather alien and perhaps even scary. After all, a field or forest is a possible source of insect bites and stings, not to mention skin rashes and scratches. As for eating the plants—well, that is really out of the question.

With this attitude toward nature, a person would not even enjoy foraging if he or she dared try it. Besides, anyone who has little knowledge about plant identification would be foolish to eat part of any wild plant.

Nevertheless, with some preparation and study, almost anyone can become a confident forager. This may mean studying several basic field guides to edible plants, or taking courses in plant identification at a nearby college, science museum, or nature center. As a result of a growing nationwide interest in wild foods, such places often offer classes in foraging, too. Classes are usually held outdoors, where people can see plants as they appear in nature, not just as they are pictured in books. No one can become an expert on wild foods overnight, but going on field trips with an experienced forager is one of the best ways to quickly gain knowledge and confidence at recognizing both safe and unsafe plants.

DANGERS, REAL AND IMAGINED

In a recent television comedy, Tarzan came home on the five o'clock vine and asked his wife what was for dinner. She told him excitedly about some new foods which she called "eggs" and "milk." But Tarzan, suspicious, asked exactly where these foods came from, and then said in alarm, "What, you expect me to eat something you found underneath a chicken, and drink something you squeezed out of a cow?"

It is fascinating to realize that such foods as eggs and milk were once in the testing stage. Humans have lived on earth for about four million years—time enough for somebody, somewhere, to have tried eating everything. There must have been a lot of trial-and-error testing and tasting. No doubt some of the trials were fatal.

In North America there are an estimated 25,000 species of plants, of which about 700 species are poisonous. Very few people die of plant poisoning, but each year in the United States doctors treat about 12,000 cases of plant poisoning, with other cases probably going unreported. Many are the result of young children eating the leaves of houseplants, or parts of shrubs or flowering plants in their own backyards. Curiously, many of the plants we choose for their flowers or other decorative value have poisonous parts. A random selection of common wild plants from a nearby field or forest would usually be less dangerous than the plants in or around our homes.

Nevertheless, some plants are poisonous. The potential dangers of poisonous plants lead to a simple rule: *Never eat part of any plant unless you have positively identified the plant and know it is edible.* This applies to all kinds of plants, including those grown in gardens and bought in stores. It may surprise you to learn that some common food plants have poisonous parts. For example, the leaves of

Among the common plants we grow in or near our homes are the yew (above), which has poisonous leaves and a poisonous seed inside each bright red fruit, and dumbcane (Dieffenbachia), which has poisonous leaves and stems.

rhubarb, potatoes, tomatoes, and eggplant are poisonous. Apple seeds contain the poison cyanide. So do the seeds inside the hard pits or "stones" of peaches, plums, nectarines, apricots, and cherries.

It is important to know that some plants have poisonous parts, and to be cautious about them. On the other hand, there is no point in exaggerating the dangers and developing *phytophobia* — fear of plants. With some exceptions, such as poison ivy, most poisonous wild plants are rather scarce, compared with the abundance of the edible wild plants described in this book.

Unreasonable fear of poisonous plants robs people of pleasure. For example, when some people hear the word "sumac," they think instantly of poison sumac. Their phytophobia, based on ignorance about plants, causes them to worry about touching the relatively rare poisonous species. In thirty years of exploring outdoors, I have yet to see poison sumac. The nonpoisonous kinds of sumac are much more common, and unlike poison sumac they have distinctive masses of red fruits that can be used to make a lemonadelike drink.

Even the word "poisonous" is misunderstood by most people. Few poisonous plants are deadly, killing people outright. A few kinds of mushrooms are quite deadly, but many poisonous plants usually cause people to throw up—the normal response of the human digestive system trying to rid itself of a poison. The accidental ingestion of one poisonous leaf or berry will probably have no noticeable effect at all. Besides, many—but not all—poisonous plant parts have a bitter, unpleasant taste. The normal reaction is to say "Yuck" and spit it out, or at least not to try a second taste.

The dangers of poisonous plants have been exaggerated, and most such plants are easy to avoid. However, only experienced foragers, after thorough and careful study, should look for the edible kinds of plants. Foragers also have a special responsibility to young children, who tend to put all sorts of objects in their mouths. Their small size also makes them more vulnerable to small amounts of poison than adults are. In fact, the greatest risk in foraging is not to people who do it with caution and common sense but to little children who try to copy their actions. It is therefore vital to warn young children that some plants can make them sick, and to insist that they never eat a berry or any other plant part without first showing it to an adult.

Before collecting dandelions or other edible plants from a lawn, find out whether the lawn has been treated with chemical poisons to rid the lawn of weeds. If it has been, the plants themselves may have absorbed some poison, and no amount of washing will make them safe to eat.

Roadsides are often rich with edible wild plants, but lead from automobile exhausts settles upon leaves and other plant parts. The more traffic there is on a street or highway, the more lead there will be on nearby plants. Too much lead in your food can be dangerous. You can remove a lot of it from plant parts by mixing one-fourth cup of vinegar with a gallon of water and washing the food in this solution. However, it is healthier, safer, and more pleasant to forage only along roads and streets that have little traffic.

Some potentially good foraging places are spoiled by being dog toilets. Bacteria on the decaying wastes might be dangerous to eat. Normally they would be killed when the food is cooked, but you'd probably be best off just avoiding places where you find dog wastes.

Several kinds of tasty plants grow in the shallow water of ponds, marshes, and streams. Here again, caution is advised: the water may be polluted. Plants which grow in polluted water may themselves be polluted. But how can you tell? The appearance of the water is not much of a clue. Muddy-looking water is sometimes perfectly safe; you may just have to wash the "good, clean dirt" off the plants you've gathered. Sparkling clear water looks fine but may contain some biocides or other harmful chemicals. In fact, the water's clarity may be partly the result of deadly chemicals that have killed off most life in the water. Even a rich growth of plants is not necessarily a clear indication that the water is safe; it may be a sign that a lot of fertilizer or sewage is being washed into the water.

The surroundings of the water are a clue to its quality. Are you a little way downstream from a factory or a housing development, or is the stream or pond in a woods or other large undisturbed area? Since you can't easily judge the safety of water by the way it looks, perhaps the best way to tell if a pond or stream is polluted is to ask a science teacher or public health official in your community.

Some edible plants grow in water which is free of harmful chemicals but which contains dangerous bacteria from sewage. To disinfect the plants you collect, buy water-purification tablets at a camping supply store. Purify a container of water by following the directions that come with the tablets. Or mix your own water-purification solution by using household chlorine bleach. Just dissolve four drops of bleach in two quarts of water. Soak the plant parts in the solution for a half-hour or so, and then rinse with fresh water.

You will probably want to wash all of the wild-plant parts you collect. If you are squeamish about accidentally eating insects, spiders, or slugs, soak the plant parts in salty water for a few minutes. This causes the little animals to flee from their hideouts.

HOW TO FORAGE

The key to safety in foraging is to be absolutely sure you know what you are eating. Learning to tell one plant from another is not difficult. You don't have to be a botanist, and you don't need to know the names of all plants in order to recognize some safe and good-tasting ones.

People often know more about plant identification than they at first realize. Even young children can recognize several kinds of plants, or plant parts, from their experiences in eating and food shopping. For instance, most people have no trouble telling a head of lettuce from a head of cabbage, or a lemon from an orange. However, identifying a plant in the wild is more difficult. For one thing, you are looking at whole plants, which is not the case in supermarkets. Also, the plants are not neatly arranged in separate labeled bins. (The prices are missing, too!) Although some wild foods grow in dense, pure clusters, others are mixed in with inedible species.

The illustrations in this book will help you spot some common, easy-to-recognize wild foods in North America. If you still have doubts about a plant's identity, look in other books. Several helpful ones are listed in the Further Reading section at the back of the book. Most libraries will have some of them and many are available in paperback editions.

As you look at a plant, note such basic important features as the shape, texture, color, and arrangement of its leaves, its height, and its habitat. After studying drawings or photographs of a plant, and especially after having looked carefully at the plant itself, you will form an *impression* of its appearance.

We all form these impressions not just of plants but also of people. If you were asked to describe a friend's face, you might not be able to remember the color of his eyes, the shape of his ears, or other details, but you would recognize your friend instantly in a crowd.

The same thing happens after you form a strong impression of an edible wild plant. You can spot it quickly, even from a moving car or bicycle. This also applies to inedible plants. For example, the appearance of poison ivy varies a lot. Poison-ivy leaves may be big or small, shiny or dull, trailing over the ground or hanging from a climbing vine. Nevertheless, once you have formed an impression of this plant you will recognize it easily and can avoid touching it.

Once your interest in wild foods is aroused, you need not wait long to satisfy your curiosity. Begin by looking in your own backyard, if you have one, or along roads and in undeveloped patches of land. You will find a greater variety of edible wild plants in such places than in wilderness areas. In fact, people living in remote forest, mountain, or desert regions may have to come to town in order to find some common edible plants.

The reason is simple: many edible wild plants thrive in sunny open areas and under environmental conditions that people unintentionally provide for them. Some edible wild plants are "pioneer" species—the first to invade such spots as construction sites, school playgrounds, fence lines, the strips between sidewalks and streets, and corners where lawn mowers or lazy gardeners don't reach. In some communities, many tons of leaves are collected and put in piles; after they decay into rich soil, they are among the best "gardens" of wild foods.

People living in suburbs have the best of all foraging worlds, with many of the same species that live in cities plus other species that require more space and special conditions. An experience I had with a suburban patch of wild strawberries illustrates some of the pleasures—and pains—of foraging. For many years I have believed that wild strawberries are an exceptional taste treat but are too small to bother picking in quantity. Then I found an extraordinary wild-strawberry patch. Covering about an acre, the strawberries were amazingly plentiful and good-sized. In a couple of brief visits, some friends and I picked several quarts and looked forward to even greater harvests, since many more berries were still ripening. For me it was the ideal berry patch—rich in fruit, poor in mosquitoes and poison ivy.

Then the bulldozer came.

Within a few hours the land was stripped of strawberries and every other living plant. This illustrates an unhappy fact about foraging: this year's lush "garden" of wild foods may be next year's home-site or parking lot.

In this case there was some consolation. The land was plowed and readied for a crop of green peppers. At least for the time being the land is part of a working farm, not just the site for another housing development. And there is hope that someday the field may be abandoned, the few surviving strawberry plants around the edges will begin to send out runners, and "my" special wild-strawberry patch will live again.

Foraging for wild food requires very little equipment: a sharp knife (for safety, take one with fold-up blades or one that is carried in a sheath), some plastic bags or other lightweight containers, and one or more books to aid you in identification. These items are easily carried in a small backpack or bicycle saddlebags. By the way, a bicycle is an ideal foraging vehicle. It is easy to spot edible plants from a bike, and stopping to collect them poses no problems. When foraging you should wear long pants to protect your legs from scratches and poison ivy.

In some places you may have to ask permission of the land-owner before foraging. Usually people are quite cooperative; they ex-

From a bicycle it is easy to see edible wild plants,
then stop and collect them.

press surprise that "those weeds are good to eat." In most city,
county, and other public parks, however, it is illegal to collect plants
of any kind.

When you find a patch of edible wild plants, it is usually wise
to leave some untouched. This may help ensure that there will be
another, perhaps larger crop of wild foods there in later years.

TO EVERYTHING THERE IS A SEASON

In supermarkets it is possible to buy some kinds of fruits and vegetables year-round. (Unfortunately this is no guarantee that they taste good year-round.) Other foods, however—for example, asparagus, rhubarb, and summer squash—are available for only a few weeks. The same is true of wild foods. Part of the fun and challenge of foraging is discovering when certain wild foods are available in your neighborhood, and making a good harvest before they are gone for another year.

Some foragers keep a notebook or journal about their discoveries. This helps remind them when their favorite wild foods are available. On the Wild Foods Harvesting Chart you will find a general guide to the seasonal availability of the edible plants discussed in this book. Of course the harvest time can vary a lot from one region to another. By mid-spring cattail flowers are well-developed in southern states, while young cattail shoots are just appearing in the North.

Once you have worked out the details for some plants in your neighborhood, you might want to make a calendar that will help alert you, year after year, when it is time to harvest the wild foods you like. Of course from year to year there are variations in the weather that affect the growth of plants, but your calendar will usually be accurate within a few days.

Within your neighborhood you will find that some wild foods ripen at different times in different places. For examples, strawberries in sunny spots usually mature before those in the shade. Those growing on a south-facing slope ripen before berries on a north-facing hillside.

Foragers use a variety of natural clues to remind themselves that certain wild foods are ready for harvesting. In southeastern New York State, where I live, the first wild-daisy blossoms delight me, both because the flowers are beautiful and because they signal that the wild strawberries are ripe. This may seem rather roundabout, but the daisy flowers are easy to see, while the wild strawberries are well hidden and easily overlooked.

Certain dead plant stalks also please foragers, because the stalks are clues to the location of future meals. Such plants as cattail, poke, Japanese knotweed, and wild asparagus have distinctive long-lasting dead stalks. They are winter and early spring reminders that new growth will soon arise from the perennial roots.

You might want to make a map of your neighborhood, indicating on it the location of such dead stalks as well as other good foraging spots you have found. Preparing a map may also prompt you to investigate a field or other foraging area you have overlooked.

EATING WILD FOODS

Some wild foods taste somewhat like common cultivated plants you have eaten already and may already like or dislike. But as Euell Gibbons has written, "Each species has a flavor, aroma, and texture all its own, and is a good food in and of itself. It doesn't have to pose as a substitute for something else."

Wild foods are well worth a try. Chances are you will find at least a few kinds of edible wild plants whose taste you will enjoy. And you will be eating nutritious food. Although information concerning their nutritional value is incomplete for many wild foods, we do know that some plentiful species are good sources of vitamins and minerals. The young shoots of poke plants, for example, contain three times the vitamin C of oranges.

Wild foods also offer other rewards, including their fresh flavor. A lot of the "fresh" food we eat is many days old, and as carefully preserved and packaged as it may be, this food cannot match the flavor of a just-picked fruit or vegetable. Unfortunately, the very freshness of wild foods may cause some people to say, "This has an odd taste."

Wild foods may have a flavor unlike anything you've ever eaten, but don't reject them just because they aren't like what you're used to. Give the new flavors a fair trial. Every wild food in this book is considered a great taste treat—by somebody. But tastes vary, and you may not agree. Or you may find a way of preparing a wild edible plant that appeals to you much more than the recipes suggested in this book. The field of wild-food cookery is wide open for experimentation, so consider the recipes here and in other books as simply a starting point.

Some foragers take pleasure in preparing complete wild-food dinners. The menu may include such main courses as freshly caught fish or seafood. You might want to try this sometime, especially if there's a fisherperson in the family or neighborhood. (Adding fish or wild game to the menu also involves knowing about state laws concerning seasons and limits, perhaps getting fishing or hunting licenses, and buying or borrowing equipment.)

Complete meals of wild foods can also be meatless, with the main course a casserole, quiche, or omelet. You need to know only a few kinds of wild edible plants in order to put together a varied menu, including dessert and beverage. It is fun to show off your skill at "living off the land" and to share the fruits of foraging as well as the good tastes. You can also accomplish this in other less elaborate ways: by adding a couple of wild greens to the lettuce in your salad; by introducing your family to a new vegetable dish; or by treating your friends to a wild-food snack or dessert.

HOW TO USE THIS BOOK

The wild plants in this book are only a small fraction of the wild foods in North America, but they are some of the most common, delicious, and easily recognized species. They are presented roughly in the order that they appear in nature, beginning with early spring. Some are available for only a few weeks; others, for several months each year. For more information, see the Wild Foods Harvesting Chart.

As you read about the wild edible plants on the following pages, you may discover that you already know some of them quite well. Or you may realize that the "weed" you recently pulled from a garden or flower bed was an edible plant. Plants like these are good starting points, especially if a recipe with one of them as a main ingredient appeals to you.

The common names of plants vary from place to place. This can be confusing, so scientific names are also given in this book. They are the names recognized by botanists. You don't have to learn them, but they may come in handy if you do research in other books about plants.

Along with some general information about each plant, there is a detailed description of where to find it, how to recognize it, what part or parts are edible, when these are available, and how to harvest them. For more information on plant identification, see the next section, How to Identify a Plant.

This book also contains over seventy delicious, easy-to-follow recipes using wild foods. There are some useful cooking tips on pages 166–167. Unfamiliar cooking terms are defined in the glossary on pages 173–174.

Finally, on pages 168–172 there are tips on preserving some kinds of wild edible plants so that the pleasure of eating wild foods can be enjoyed all year long.

How to Identify a Plant

Each plant in this book can be identified by where it is found (distribution and habitat) and by its appearance (leaves, flowers, fruit, and stems). To positively identify a plant, check to be sure the specimen you have fits all of the criteria given in the Finding, Recognizing, and Caution sections about the plant in this book.

FINDING

🌿 *Distribution.* For each plant, check this section to see whether it occurs in your state. The wild foods in this book occur in many or all of the original forty-eight states; some grow in southern Alaska and in Hawaii. Since this book is an introduction, however, some fine-tasting wild plants of more limited range have been omitted. These include cactus fruits of the Southwest, and the persimmon of the central and southeastern states. (See the list of books in Further Reading for details about these and other regional wild foods.)

🌿 *Habitat.* Just because a plant grows in your state doesn't mean you will find it in your neighborhood. Check the description of the plant's habitat to find out more about the kinds of places it lives; then look in such places.

RECOGNIZING

The photographs and drawings will help you recognize the plants. You may want to take this book along on your foraging trips, and compare the illustrations in it directly with living plants. Look at plants in the wild and compare their characteristics with information in this book about:

🌿 *Appearance.* This section provides a description of the general appearance of the plant.

Leaves. This section mentions such features as the type of leaf and the characteristic leaf arrangement, shape, margin, and color. For example, leaves can be arranged along a stem either opposite each other or alternately. They can be divided into lobes or edged with a toothlike pattern, or they can have neither lobes nor teeth. They can be simple or compound (divided into leaflets). Leaflets of compound leaves may be either of two basic shapes. Pinnate compound leaves have leaflets placed in an arrangement similar to that of a feather. Palmate compound leaves have leaflets in an arrangement similar to the spread-out fingers of a hand, or an open fan.

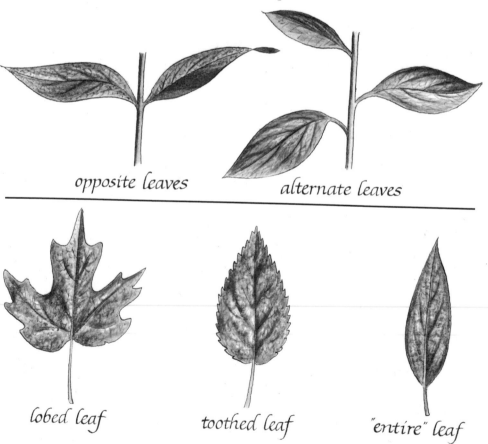

opposite leaves   alternate leaves

lobed leaf   toothed leaf   "entire" leaf

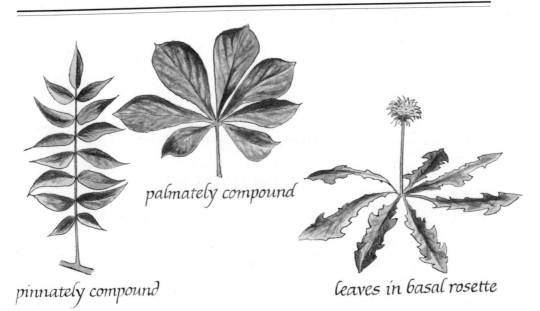

palmately compound

pinnately compound

leaves in basal rosette

🌿 *Flowers.* This describes such features as the number, color, shape, and arrangement of the flowers. Some of the possible arrangements of a plant's flowers (and you will find examples of these in this book) are as follows:

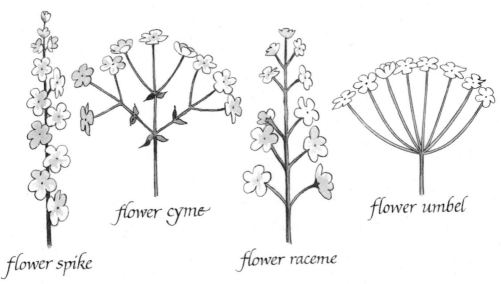

flower cyme

flower umbel

flower spike

flower raceme

🌿 *Fruit.* This describes such features as the type of fruit, size, color, and arrangement.

🌿 *Stems.* This describes such features as the appearance, height, and color of the stem. Several of the plants in this book are stemless, though they may have flower stalks which resemble stems. Also, some have rhizomes—underground food-storage stems.

CAUTION

If a plant is similar in appearance to another species, specific examples will be given under this heading to help you tell the edible plants from the inedible or poisonous ones. The illustrations will clearly distinguish any similar plants.

In identifying plants, one common-sense rule is worth repeating: *Never eat part of any plant unless you have positively identified it and know for sure that it is edible.*

Wild Foods Harvesting Chart

This chart shows when parts of the edible plants described in this book are normally available. An asterisk (*) means the harvesting season of that part of the plant can be extended. You will find details about this in the text about specific plants.

PLANT	SPRING	SUMMER	FALL	WINTER
maple	sap (early)			
dandelion	leaves*			
	leaf crowns	leaf crowns		
	roots	roots	roots	roots
				(in some areas)
plantain	leaves*			

PLANT	SPRING	SUMMER	FALL	WINTER
Japanese knotweed	shoots* stems*			
poke	shoots* leaves from shoots*			
cattail	core of shoots flower spikes rhizomes	pollen rhizomes	rhizomes	rhizomes
wild strawberry	leaves	fruit leaves	leaves (early)	
sheep sorrel	leaves (late)	leaves	leaves (early)	
watercress	leaves and stems	leaves and stems	leaves and stems	leaves and stems
elderberry		flowers fruit	fruit (early)	
milkweed	flowers (late)	flowers seed pods		
wild mint	leaves (late)	leaves	leaves (early)	
wild raspberries and blackberries		fruit		
daylily	tubers	tubers flower buds and flowers	tubers	tubers (in some areas)
lamb's-quarters	leaves and stems (late)	leaves and stems	seeds, leaves and stems (early)	
purslane	leaves and stems (late)	leaves and stems	leaves and stems (early)	
wild blueberry		fruit		
sumac		fruit	fruit (early)	
wild grape	leaves (late)	leaves (early) fruit	fruit (early)	

Maple

❧ COMMON NAMES ❧

sugar maple, red maple, silver maple, broad-leaf maple, Rocky Mountain maple, and big-leaf maple are some native North American species.

❧ SCIENTIFIC NAME ❧

Acer saccharum *is the well-known sugar maple.*

Contrary to popular belief, maple syrup can come from states other than Vermont and from trees other than the sugar maple. Euell Gibbons tested six maple species and found no significant difference in syrup quantity or quality. Even if there are some differences between species, many people in the United States can experience the pleasures of making their own delicious maple syrup. If some kind of maple tree grows near you and the early spring climate includes a period of freezing nights and thawing days (usually some time between February and April), you will probably be successful at making maple syrup.

Syrup making requires more effort and equipment than the usual kinds of foraging, for only a small part of the sap is made of the sugar and other substances that give maple syrup its special flavor; as a result, thirty to forty pints of water have to be boiled away in order to get one pint of syrup. But syrup making offers some special re-

Sugar maple leaves have a few large teeth on their
edges, and turn bright yellow or orange in the autumn.

wards. For one thing, the end result is not a wild vegetable that few
people know; maple syrup is widely known as a delicious and luxu-
rious product. The sap itself is a symbol of spring. Collecting it outdoors after spending the cold winter indoors is part of the fun of
making your own syrup.

FINDING MAPLES

❧ *Distribution.* Sugar maple grows in the Northeast, west to North
Dakota, and south to Georgia and eastern Texas. The ranges of red

maple and silver maple also occur in the Northeast but extend farther south, to Florida. Broad-leaf maple grows in southern Alaska and
all along the West Coast. Rocky Mountain maple occurs in western
mountains from southern Alaska to Arizona.

✻ *Habitat.* The habitat varies from species to species. Sugar maple
grows in fairly moist forests and is also widely used as a shade tree
near houses and along streets and roads. The Norway maple, which
was imported from Europe, is also planted along city and suburban
streets. Red maple and silver maple thrive in such wet places as
swamps and stream banks.

RECOGNIZING MAPLES

✻ *Appearance.* Most maple species are medium-to-large trees.
✻ *Leaves.* With the exception of the box elder, all maples have
simple leaves that grow opposite each other, are lobed, and have
toothed edges. Sugar-maple leaves are usually five-lobed with large
pointed teeth.
✻ *Flowers.* Maples have clusters of small flowers; sugar-maple
flowers are yellow and have long stems.
✻ *Fruit.* Maple seeds grow in pairs, each with a "wing."
✻ *Stems.* Young sugar-maple trees have fairly smooth gray bark. The
gray-brown bark of older trees is broken into vertical ridges and
sometimes flakes off.

HARVESTING MAPLES

Maple sap flows upward in trees during days when Fahrenheit
temperatures are in the forties, after nights when temperatures are in
the twenties. In northern regions these conditions usually occur in
March and early April. Farther south, a thaw in January or February
may produce a few days of heavy sap flow. Also, the beginning and
duration of spring sap flow in maples varies from year to year, so it is

MAPLE *Acer*

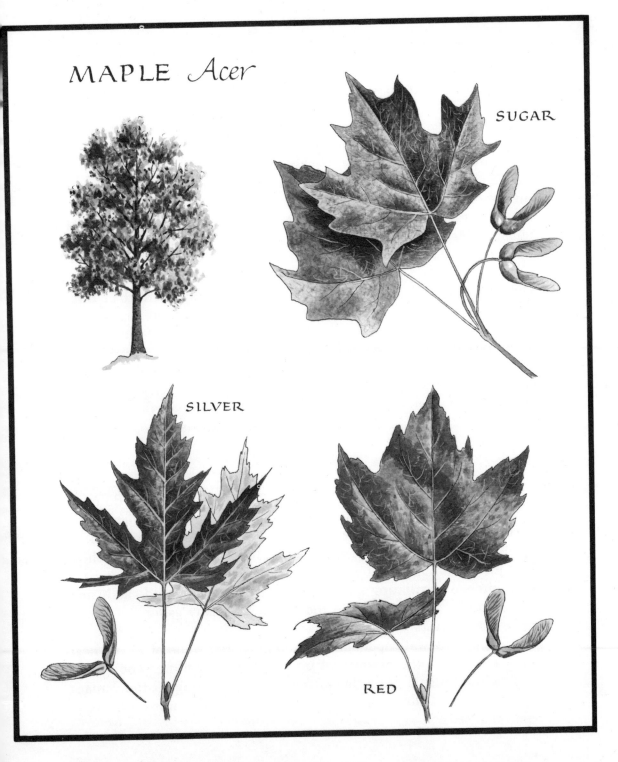

SUGAR

SILVER

RED

wise to have all your equipment ready and the trees located before-hand.

The first thing to do is find at least one maple tree you can tap. You will probably find maple trees near your home. If you don't have any in your yard, your neighbors may be willing to let you tap their maple trees, especially if they are promised a little of the resulting syrup.

The maples should be fairly big—at least 35 inches in circumference. (Measure with a flexible measuring tape or a piece of string that you can later compare with a ruler or yardstick.)

Beware of tapping too many trees. One good-sized maple may yield 30 to 40 gallons of sap each spring. If you tap more than three or four trees, a lot of sap may go to waste unless you are prepared to boil hundreds of gallons. Read all the way through the following instructions to get an idea of the amount of work and heat needed to process maple sap. You may choose to tap a dozen trees or just one. Of course it is especially rewarding to make many pints of syrup—perhaps with your own homemade "brand name" label—but small-scale syrup making is also fun and much less expensive.

CAUTION

If you choose to boil many gallons of sap, it is best to do most of this outdoors and just do the final cooking on the kitchen stove. According to Christopher Letts, foraging consultant for this book, a family in New Jersey boiled about 400 gallons of sap in their kitchen. This produced huge amounts of water vapor, but the people thought their kitchen ventilating fan would pull most of it outdoors. Their plan seemed to work well, and they produced many gallons of home-made maple syrup.

Then the wallpaper started peeling off the walls of rooms near the kitchen, and the plaster fell off the kitchen ceiling. The family made a lot of maple syrup, but if the cost of repairing all the damage is taken into account, the syrup was probably the most expensive ever produced.

Equipment

Here is a list of the equipment you'll need:

1. a brace (hand-operated drill) with drill bit a half-inch in diameter.
2. hollow spiles (tubes), about 3 to 5 inches long and a half-inch across. Some hardware stores sell metal spiles, but you can make your own from branches of elderberry or sumac (both described later in this book), by sawing off the appropriate length and then using coat-hanger wire or other sturdy wire to push out all of the soft pith, leaving a hollow wooden tube.
3. a hammer and some nails 1 1/2 to 2 inches long.
4. plastic or metal buckets for collecting sap. You can also make buckets from one-gallon cans (often available in great numbers from restaurants or school cafeterias). With a can opener remove any remaining tops. Wash thoroughly. With a hammer and nail punch holes near the top on opposite sides; then attach a length of sturdy wire to the holes in order to make a handle for the bucket.
5. aluminum foil.
6. one or more large pans.
7. a candy thermometer.
8. a large spoon or ladle.
9. a fine-mesh strainer or sieve.
10. jars with lids for storing the finished syrup.

To boil large amounts of sap, you will need an outdoor fireplace. Use an existing concrete or brick fireplace or a temporary one made of bricks or cinder blocks. Also, a lot of wood will be needed to keep the sap boiling. It need not be the finest of firewood; fallen tree limbs, old boards, scrap lumber, and wood from packing cases will do quite well.

Collecting

The time of heavy sap flow in maples varies from year to year because it depends on the changeable weather of early spring. Most of

The sap bucket (left) was made from a one-gallon can, and the spile from an elderberry branch. A temporary outdoor fireplace (below) may be needed to boil large quantities of maple sap.

it may occur in a few days, or it may flow in an off-and-on pattern for a month. A big maple can yield sap for two or three buckets at once. If only one bucket is used, put it on the tree's south side. The sap should be collected daily, and perhaps two or three times a day at the peak of sap flow when the buckets fill quickly.

With the brace and bit, drill a slightly-upward-slanting hole, two to three inches deep, about three to four feet above the ground. With the hammer, gently tap a spile into the hole. It should fit snugly so the sap drips out the hole, not down the side of the tree. A few inches above the spile, drive a nail partway into the tree and hang the bucket's handle on it. Make a cover of aluminum foil to keep out rain and insects. When the sap stops flowing or when you have gathered all you want, remove the spiles and nails. The tree will gradually grow new wood over the taphole. To get maximum flow of sap, drill new tapholes each year.

Cooking

For best results, use large shallow pans—the more surface area from which water vapor can escape, the better. Bring the sap to a boil and keep it boiling. The remaining liquid will gradually change from clear to light brown. Spoon off the foamy scum that appears on the surface.

When a batch of syrup has lost most of its water it will begin to thicken. It may also begin to boil over the sides of the pan. To avoid this, drop a few small pieces of butter or drops of cream or cooking oil into the liquid. Watch the sap closely during this last stage, because just a few minutes of overcooking will leave you with a scorched pan and no syrup.

Maple syrup is "done" when it boils at 7° F above the temperature of boiling water. At or near sea level, this would be about 219° F (212° + 7° = 219°). If the altitude where you live is considerably above sea level, use a candy thermometer to determine the temperature at which fresh water boils. Add seven degrees and you will have the correct temperature at which to remove your syrup from the heat.

Pour the syrup through a fine-mesh strainer to remove such impurities as bits of bark and insects before pouring it into jars. To prevent the growth of mold, seal the jars tightly and store them in a cool cupboard. Once opened, however, they should be stored in the refrigerator.

If you want maple candy, boil the syrup longer. Put a small quantity of syrup in a large pot. The pot should be no more than one-third full. This helps reduce the danger of the syrup boiling over. Cookbooks disagree about the ideal temperature to stop cooking maple candy, but one test for doneness is to drop a bit of syrup from a spoon into cold water. It should form into the shape of a ball that feels soft to your fingers. (Remove the syrup from the heat to check this; otherwise it may boil beyond the soft-ball stage.) Pour the thick syrup into a bowl and beat with an eggbeater or an electric mixer until it becomes creamy. Then pour it into molds—muffin tins work well—greased with cooking oil, and let cool.

RECIPES

Besides the traditional uses of maple syrup—on pancakes and waffles—there are other possibilities below, and in other cookbooks.

Maple Divinity Candy

INGREDIENTS	EQUIPMENT
4 cups maple syrup, or 2 cups syrup and 2 cups sugar	measuring cup
	heavy saucepan
4 egg whites	candy thermometer
1 cup chopped walnuts or hickory nuts	eggbeater or electric mixer
	large knife
	teaspoon
	waxed paper

Yield: about 36 pieces of candy

1. Heat the syrup in the saucepan until it reaches the soft-ball stage when dropped into cold water (about 240° F on the candy thermometer).
2. Beat the egg whites until they form stiff peaks.
3. Pour the hot syrup slowly into the whites and continue to beat slowly until the mixture forms stiff peaks.
4. Add the nuts and mix them in thoroughly.
5. Drop teaspoonfuls of candy onto a sheet of waxed paper.
6. Let the candy cool and harden at room temperature or in the refrigerator before serving.

NOTE: For best results make this on a cool, dry day, not during humid weather.

Maple Bread Pudding

INGREDIENTS

6–8 slices stale bread (to make
   4 cups bread pieces)

2 eggs

3 cups milk

2/3 cup maple syrup

1/8 teaspoon nutmeg

1/4 teaspoon cinnamon

1/2 cup raisins

1 tablespoon butter

1 pint heavy cream

EQUIPMENT

large mixing bowl

eggbeater or electric mixer

measuring cups

measuring spoons

8" × 12" × 2" baking dish

Yield: 6 servings

1. Use day-old bread if it is home-baked. If the bread contains preservatives let it age longer, but don't let it get hard.
2. Cut off the crusts and break the bread into pieces.
3. Preheat the oven to 375° F.
4. In the large bowl break the eggs, add the milk, and beat briefly.
5. Add the maple syrup, nutmeg, and cinnamon. Mix thoroughly, using eggbeater or electric mixer.
6. Add the raisins and bread and continue mixing until all ingredients are blended.
7. Pour into the baking dish.
8. Dot the top with butter and bake in the preheated oven for an hour.
9. Serve warm with cream, or whipped cream.

Maple Baked Apples

INGREDIENTS	EQUIPMENT
8 large tart apples, unpeeled	apple corer
1/2 cup seedless raisins	measuring cup
1/2 cup chopped walnuts or hickory nuts	small mixing bowl
	baking dish with cover
4 tablespoons lemon juice	measuring spoons
1 1/2 cups maple syrup	tablespoon
2 tablespoons butter	

Yield: 8 apples

1. Preheat the oven to 375° F.
2. Wash and core the apples, leaving the skin on.

3. Mix the raisins and nuts together; then fill the centers of the apples with this mixture.

4. Put the apples in the baking dish. Pour the lemon juice and the syrup over them.

5. Put about 1/4 tablespoon butter on top of each apple.

6. Cover and bake in the preheated oven for 40 minutes, occasionally spooning the maple syrup from the dish over the apples.

7. Serve either warm or cooled, with the syrup that remains in the baking dish.

Dandelion

❦ COMMON NAMES ❧
blowball, lion's tooth, milk witch

❦ SCIENTIFIC NAME ❧
Taraxacum officinale *is the most common and widespread species.*

Beautiful and useful, the dandelion is one of the best-known plants on earth. Bees make honey from its pollen, birds eat its abundant seeds, and people enjoy blowing on the seed clusters—"blowballs"—to send the seed-bearing "parachutes" on their way. People also make a fine wine from its flowers, as well as meals from its leaves and roots.

When a seed sprouts, the new dandelion plant sends its root deep underground. Because of this deep root, dandelions are difficult weeds to get rid of in a lawn, where they compete with grasses for sunlight and space. To some people, therefore, the dandelion is an obnoxious weed. To others, it is a pretty sight in spring and a tasty source of vitamin A, calcium, and potassium.

The edible stage of dandelion leaves occurs before
the plant's showy yellow flowers appear.

FINDING DANDELIONS

🌿 *Distribution*. Dandelion species occur over most of North America, including parts of the Arctic.

🌿 *Habitat*. Dandelions can be found on lawns and roadsides, as well as in fields, schoolyards, and gardens.

RECOGNIZING DANDELIONS

Appearance. A stemless, low-growing plant with bright yellow flower clusters.

Leaves. Arranged in a rosette at the base of the plant, the dark-green leaves are deeply lobed and toothed in a jagged pattern.

Flowers. The flower-bearing stalk is hollow and oozes a milky sap when cut. Each "petal" of a dandelion flower is a complete flower.

Fruit. A hundred or more small olive or brown seeds attached to parachutes make up each blowball.

HARVESTING DANDELIONS

Although dandelions are available from early spring to late fall, the plant is good-tasting only during the early spring, unless special steps (see below) are taken in harvesting or preparation. The ideal harvesting time is early spring, when new leaves sprout from the perennial roots. The greens can be plucked until flower stalks appear. After that, the chemistry of the leaves changes and they become tough and bitter-tasting.

To harvest roots and leaf crowns—the underground bases of the leaves—dig with a sturdy trowel or a shovel. If you don't plan to use the root, just cut the cluster of leaf crowns from it, replace the soil, and the root will eventually produce new growth.

To extend the harvesting season of dandelion leaves, cover mature plants with lawn clippings, newspapers, cardboard, black plastic, or any other material that shuts off the sunlight. In a week or so the leaves will be blanched yellowish-white, quite tender, and as tasty as young spring leaves.

CAUTION

Beware of collecting dandelions from places where plant-killing chemicals may have been used. Don't forage in such places.

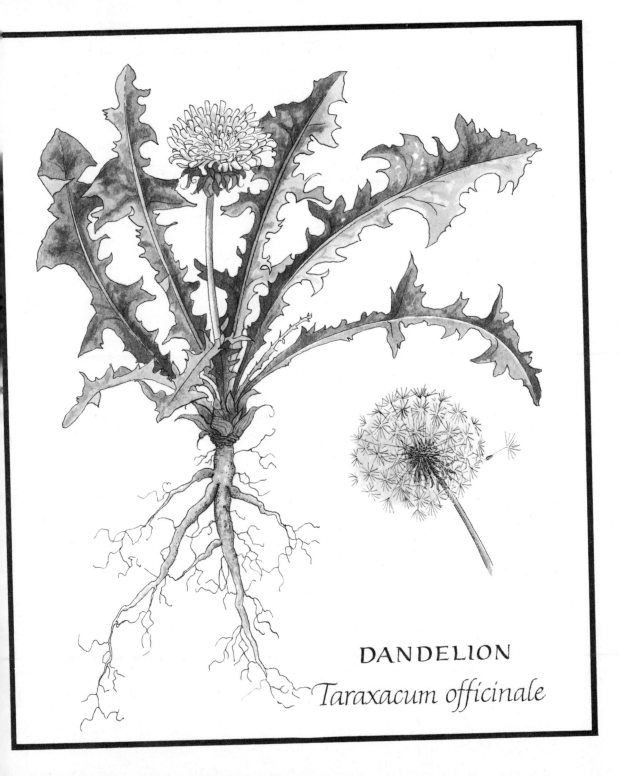

DANDELION

Taraxacum officinale

RECIPES

Young leaves can be eaten raw in salads, as can the leaf crowns and leaves that have been blanched. Older leaves and roots make tasty cooked vegetables, either boiled or steamed (see Cooking Tips, page 166), though you may have to change the cooking water once or twice to get rid of some bitter flavor.

Dandelion Salad

INGREDIENTS	EQUIPMENT
2 eggs	small saucepan
2 cups young dandelion leaves	measuring cups
2 cups lettuce	large salad bowl
4 scallions, sliced	measuring spoons
1/2 green pepper, coarsely chopped	sharp knife
1 cup cherry tomatoes, halved	grater
1/3 pound Swiss cheese, coarsely grated	
1/4 teaspoon salt	
1/8 teaspoon pepper	
3 tablespoons salad oil	
4 tablespoons wine vinegar	

Yield: 4 servings

1. Boil water in the saucepan and add the eggs. Reduce the heat and let the eggs simmer for about 10 minutes.
2. Remove the eggs and let them cool, but make a break in their

shells with a spoon before they cool completely, so they'll be easier to peel later.

3. Carefully wash the dandelion leaves and lettuce, and tear into small pieces. Put these and the scallions and green pepper into a large salad bowl.

4. Add the tomatoes and Swiss cheese.

5. Add salt and pepper. Then toss the ingredients gently.

6. Mix the oil and vinegar together and pour over the salad. Toss gently.

7. Peel and slice the eggs, arrange the slices on top of the salad, and serve.

Dandelion-Root Tea

INGREDIENTS

5–6 dandelion roots

EQUIPMENT

vegetable brush or an old
    toothbrush
vegetable peeler
cookie sheet
blender or coffee grinder

Yield: 4 cups

1. Use the vegetable brush to scrub the roots clean; then scrape off as much skin as possible.

2. Place the roots on a cookie sheet in a 300° F oven for about 4 hours. When thoroughly dry, the roots should be dark brown in the center when you snap them in two.

3. Grind the roots as finely as possible in a blender or coffee grinder.

4. Mix 1 teaspoon of ground dandelion root with a cup of hot water for each serving. Let it steep for about 3 minutes; then strain out the dandelion particles. Add cream or milk and sugar if you like.

Dandelion-Crown Omelet

INGREDIENTS

1 cup dandelion leaf crowns

3 tablespoons butter

6 eggs at room temperature

3 teaspoons cold water

salt and pepper to taste

EQUIPMENT

frying pan or omelet pan

measuring cup

measuring spoons

mixing bowl

wire whisk

spatula

Yield: 2 to 4 servings

1. Wash the crowns thoroughly and let drain.
2. Melt 2 tablespoons of butter in a frying pan. Sauté the dandelion crowns for about 5 minutes; then set aside, keeping them warm.
3. Break the eggs into a bowl, add the cold water, and beat with a wire whisk for a few seconds, just until the yolks and whites are combined.
4. Melt the remaining tablespoon of butter in a frying pan or omelet pan until it sizzles but does not burn (if it turns brown the pan is too hot). Pour in the eggs and cook slowly over low heat until the bottom begins to cook. Then add the dandelion crowns.
5. Lift the edges of the omelet with a spatula so that the still-liquid egg mixture can run under.
6. Continue cooking over low heat. Shake the pan back and forth to keep the omelet from sticking.
7. When the omelet is firm except for a slightly soft middle portion, use the spatula to fold one side over the other. Tilt the pan so that the omelet slides onto a warm serving plate. Serve at once. Salt and pepper to taste.

Dandelion Greens in Cream Sauce

INGREDIENTS

4 cups young dandelion greens

4 slices bacon

1/2 cup sugar

1/2 teaspoon salt

1 tablespoon cornstarch

1 egg

1/4 cup vinegar

1 cup cream

EQUIPMENT

paper towels

frying pan

medium saucepan

measuring cups

measuring spoons

eggbeater or electric mixer

Yield: 4 servings

1. Wash the dandelion leaves carefully, pat dry on paper towels, and chop coarsely.

2. Fry the bacon until crisp. Drain it on paper towels, and reserve the bacon fat in the pan.

3. In a saucepan combine the sugar, salt, and cornstarch, and mix well.

4. Beat the egg, add it and the vinegar to the saucepan, and mix well.

5. Crumble the bacon into little pieces and add it, the cream, and the reserved bacon fat to the saucepan.

6. Cook the sauce over medium heat for several minutes, until it begins to thicken.

7. Pour the hot sauce over the dandelion greens and mix until the leaves are wilted. Serve at once.

Plantain

❦ COMMON NAMES ❧

Narrow-leaved plantain is also called ribgrass, ribwort, and English plantain; broad-leaved plantain is called common plantain, dooryard plantain, and white-man's-foot.

❦ SCIENTIFIC NAMES ❧

Plantago lanceolata *(narrow-leaved plantain)*
Plantago major *(broad-leaved plantain)*

This group of plants (genus *Plantago*) is not related to the tropical plant with bananalike fruit which has the same common name. Worldwide, there are about 200 species in the *Plantago* group. The species shown here were both brought from Europe. Their leaves press close to the ground, shading out grasses, so they are considered pests of lawns.

Even though there is a native kind of broad-leaved plantain *(Plantago rugellii)*, Indians in eastern North America gave the introduced species *(Plantago major)* the name "white-man's-foot." The Indians reportedly observed that "wherever a European had walked, this plant grew in his footsteps."

Broad-leaved plantain leaves are best at this stage,
before the flower spikes develop.

FINDING PLANTAIN

🌿 *Distribution.* Plantain species occur in all 50 states.

🌿 *Habitat.* Plantain can be found on lawns, roadsides, and play-grounds, and in vacant lots and sidewalk cracks.

RECOGNIZING PLANTAIN

🌿 *Appearance.* Low-growing, stemless plants with inconspicuous flowers.

🌿 *Leaves.* Plantain leaves have deep parallel veins running the length of the leaf, and they grow in a rosette. Leaves of narrow-leaved plantain are long, slender, and pointed, shaped like a lance (hence the name *lanceolata*). Broad-leaved plantain leaves are shaped like spoons without handles.

❧ *Flowers.* Broad-leaved plantain has small green flowers arranged along the length of the slender flower stalk. Narrow-leaved plantain flowers, also inconspicuous, grow in a bushy cluster atop the slender flower stalk.

❧ *Fruit.* Abundant brown seeds develop inside tiny capsules.

HARVESTING PLANTAIN

Plantain is available from early spring until autumn, but is most edible in the spring when its leaves are fresh and tender. Simply pinch off the leaves at their bases and collect them in a plastic bag. As time passes, and especially when the flower spikes appear, the leaves become tough and bitter. As with dandelions, you can cause plantain to produce tender new growth. One way is to cut off all the mature leaves and wait for new ones to appear. Another is to cover plants with lawn clippings, black plastic, newspapers—anything that shuts them off from sunlight. After a few days check the condition of the plantain leaves. They will gradually lose most of their coloring, and will gain tenderness and a more pleasing flavor.

Also watch for special conditions that may provide a later-than-usual harvest of plantain. One August, I found a huge crop of young broad-leaved plantain in a wheat field. It had begun to grow after the wheat was harvested and full sunlight was able to reach the soil.

CAUTION

Remember that poisons are sometimes applied to lawns in order to kill plantain and other weeds. Don't forage in such places.

PLANTAIN *Plantago*

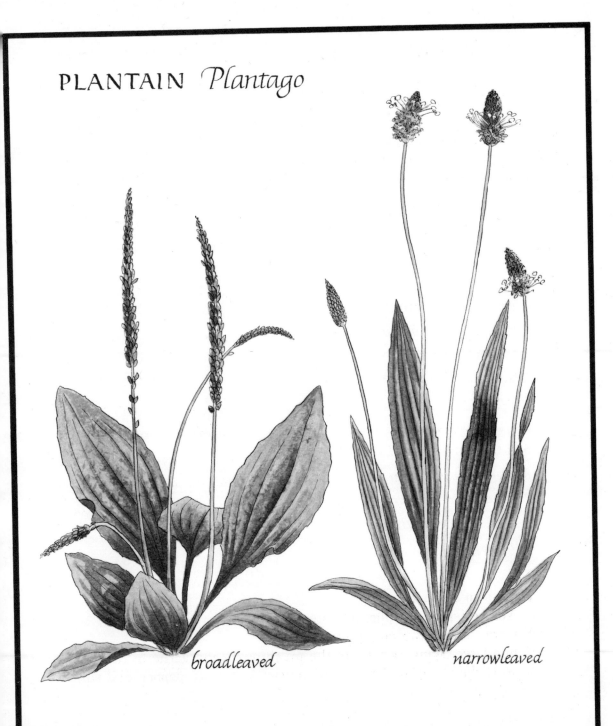

broadleaved

narrowleaved

RECIPES

The most common use of plantains is as a spring green, with the raw leaves chopped and mixed with dandelions and other plants in a salad. Another way to prepare plantain is as a cooked vegetable, alone or with other leafy green vegetables (see Cooking Tips, page 166).

Beef-Plantain Rolls

INGREDIENTS	EQUIPMENT
4 cups packed plantain leaves	measuring cup
1/2 pound fresh mushrooms, sliced	vegetable steamer
1 large clove garlic, peeled and minced	medium saucepan
3 tablespoons olive oil	sharp knife
1 teaspoon summer savory	cover for frying pan
salt and pepper to taste	measuring spoons
6–8 thin slices round steak	large frying pan
3 tablespoons butter	small mixing bowl
2 tablespoons cooking oil	3 feet kite string or button thread
1–1 1/2 cups red wine	
1 tablespoon flour	

Yield: 6 to 8 servings

1. After washing the plantain, steam or boil it for a few minutes, until tender. Drain thoroughly, then chop.
2. In a large frying pan, sauté the mushrooms and garlic in the olive oil. Add the chopped plantain. Season with the salt, pepper, and summer savory.

3. Put the plantain-mushroom mixture on the meat slices, roll them up (like rugs) and tie up each end with string or thread.

4. In the same frying pan melt 2 tablespoons butter and add the cooking oil. Brown the meat rolls on all sides.

5. Add the wine (enough to go about halfway up the side of the frying pan). Cover the skillet and simmer until the meat is tender, between 15 and 30 minutes.

6. Remove the stuffed meat rolls to a heated serving dish and cut off the strings.

7. Turn up the heat and rapidly boil the sauce in the pan.

8. In a bowl, blend the remaining tablespoon of butter and a tablespoon of flour. Stir as you gradually add this to the sauce. Once the sauce has thickened, pour it over the meat rolls and serve.

Puréed Plantain

INGREDIENTS	EQUIPMENT
6 cups packed plantain leaves	*measuring cup*
2 tablespoons butter	*vegetable steamer*
1/2 cup skim-milk ricotta cheese	*medium saucepan*
1/2 teaspoon freshly ground nutmeg	*measuring spoons*
salt and pepper to taste	*sharp knife*
	large frying pan

Yield: 4 to 6 servings

1. Wash the plantain, then steam or boil it for a few minutes, until tender.

2. In a large skillet, sauté the plantain in butter, then mix in the cheese.

3. Heat it thoroughly, add the nutmeg, salt, and pepper and serve immediately.

Japanese Knotweed

🌿 COMMON NAMES 🌿

giant knotweed, American bamboo, wild rhubarb

🌿 SCIENTIFIC NAME 🌿

Polygonum cuspidatum

A native of Japan, this knotweed was brought to North America about 1870. Considered a nuisance in parks and gardens, it is difficult to wipe out and continues to spread across the nation.

Japanese knotweed is related to about thirty other kinds of knotweed (most of them small plants) that are North American natives. One of these, *Polygonum alpinum*, grows in Alaska and western Canada, where its bright red stems are used as a substitute for rhubarb—as are the stems of Japanese knotweed.

One good-sized clump of Japanese knotweed can produce food for many meals. The plant has a mildly tart flavor and can be prepared as a vegetable or as a fruit in pies, jams, and sauces.

FINDING JAPANESE KNOTWEED

🌿 *Distribution.* Japanese knotweed grows in the Northeast, south to the Carolinas, west to Iowa and Minnesota (and perhaps beyond).

🌿 *Habitat.* You will find Japanese knotweed along roadsides and in fields and abandoned gardens.

Young knotweed stems produce desserts with a rhubarblike tang.

RECOGNIZING JAPANESE KNOTWEED

❧ *Appearance.* Tall plants with good-sized leaves, forming dense thickets.

❧ *Leaves.* Up to 6 inches long, the leaves have broad bases and are sharply pointed at the tip. They are arranged alternately on the stem.

❧ *Flowers.* Clusters (racemes) of small greenish-white flowers grow in the angles between the stems and leaves.

❧ *Fruit.* The seeds are small and inconspicuous.

❧ *Stems.* Up to ten feet tall, the stems are mottled green and hollow. They are also divided into sections by enlarged joints, like bamboo. Each joint is covered with a papery sheath.

HARVESTING JAPANESE KNOTWEED

In the spring, watch for the stout new shoots, called sprouts, coming up among the dead stalks. Cut them off at ground level before their leaves unfurl completely. The sprouts are edible as vegetables until they grow to be about a foot in height. The sprouts don't all develop at the same time, and you may be able to find short sprouts at the bases of others that have grown several feet tall.

The young stems, up to about three feet tall, are also edible in pies, tarts, and sauces but are prepared in different ways. Select those that are still somewhat tender. You should be able to cut them easily with a moderately sharp knife. If you have trouble chopping them into pieces, the cooked stalks will leave you with a mouthful of unchewable fibers—something like eating toothbrush bristles.

You can extend the harvesting season of Japanese knotweed by cutting off mature stalks to stimulate new sprout growth.

You will find knotweed sprouts at the base of old stalks.

JAPANESE KNOTWEED
Polygonum cuspidatum

flowers

shoot with young leaves

sprouts

RECIPES

Steam knotweed sprouts (see Cooking Tips, page 166) and serve hot with butter, salt, and other seasonings. You can also chill the cooked parts and serve them later with a salad dressing or mayonnaise.

Japanese-Knotweed Pie

INGREDIENTS	EQUIPMENT
1 1/2 cups sugar	sharp knife
1/4 cup flour	paring knife or peeler
3/4 teaspoon nutmeg	measuring cup
3 eggs	measuring spoons
4 cups peeled* and chopped young knotweed stalks	small mixing bowl
	large mixing bowl
1 store-bought or homemade double-crust pastry for a 9-inch pie	eggbeater or electric mixer
	9-inch pie plate

*Peel off most of the outer purple rind, being careful not to remove so much that you have nothing left.

Yield: one 9-inch pie
1. Preheat the oven to 400° F.
2. In a small mixing bowl, combine the sugar, flour, and nutmeg.
3. In a large bowl, beat the eggs, then add the flour-sugar mixture and the chopped knotweed. Mix thoroughly.
4. Pour this filling into the unbaked pie crust.
5. Dot the filling with butter, then cover with the top crust.
6. Join the edges of the top and bottom crust by squeezing the dough with your fingers. Press once again all around the edge of the pie with the tines of a fork to make a tight seal and an attractive border.

7. Make a few knife slits in the top crust to allow steam to escape.
8. Bake in the preheated oven for about 50 minutes. Let the pie cool somewhat before serving.

Knotweed-Sprout Casserole

INGREDIENTS

about 20 knotweed sprouts

salt and pepper to taste

1/2 cup heavy cream

1/4 cup grated Parmesan cheese

2/3 cup bread crumbs

2 tablespoons melted butter
  or margarine

EQUIPMENT

vegetable steamer

medium saucepan

1-quart baking dish

measuring cup

measuring spoons

small mixing bowl

Yield: 4 servings

1. Preheat the oven to 400° F.
2. Steam the knotweed sprouts until tender. Drain and then arrange them in the bottom of a well-greased 1-quart baking dish.
3. Season with salt and pepper. Pour the cream over all.
4. In the mixing bowl blend the Parmesan cheese and bread crumbs with the butter. Sprinkle this mixture over the casserole.
5. Bake in the preheated oven for about 20 minutes, or until the top is lightly browned. Serve immediately.

Poke

✍ COMMON NAMES ✍

pokeweed, pokum, inkberry, scoke, pigeon berry

SCIENTIFIC NAME
✍ Phytolacca americana ✍

Poke is native to North America and was a popular Indian food. Both here and in Europe some people grow it deliberately in their gardens. It is especially popular in the South, where you can sometimes buy poke sprouts in food markets. The young shoots taste something like asparagus, but have a distinctive flavor of their own.

According to historians, many soldiers in the Civil War used poke as a source of ink with which to write letters home. They squeezed red juice from the berries, and this is the origin of one of the plant's many names: inkberry.

FINDING POKE

✍ *Distribution.* Poke grows in the eastern United States, west to Minnesota and Texas.
✍ *Habitat.* Poke grows along roadsides and fences and in thickets, vacant lots, and community leaf mulch piles.

The only edible parts of the poke plant are these sprouts which arise near the dead stalks of the previous year's growth.

RECOGNIZING POKE

Appearance. A tall weed with conspicuous purple berries.

Leaves. Simple, alternate, and lance-shaped; they are usually five to nine inches long, with a long leaf-stalk.

Flowers. Clusters (racemes) of small greenish-white flowers (each with five petals).

Fruit. Several black seeds develop within each berry, which is first green, then red, and finally a deep purple.

Stems. Up to eight feet tall, the stems are hollow. They sometimes branch. Mature stems have a deep purple color. Grayish-white dead stems mark the places where new sprouts will arise from the perennial roots in the spring.

CAUTION

With the exception of the young shoots and the young leaves on them, all parts of the poke plant contain some poison. The mature stalks and leaves, the seeds within the berries, and the big roots are all dangerous to eat. The poisonous compound phytolaccin is most concentrated in the roots.

HARVESTING POKE

In the spring, look within a few inches of last year's dead poke stalks for new sprouts to appear. Harvest them when they are no more than eight inches tall, and before their leaves are completely unfurled. Cut the sprouts off at ground level. To avoid getting any poke root, don't cut below ground.

A good-sized poke root sends up many sprouts, so it is easy to harvest enough for a meal from just a few plants.

POKE *Phytolacca americana*

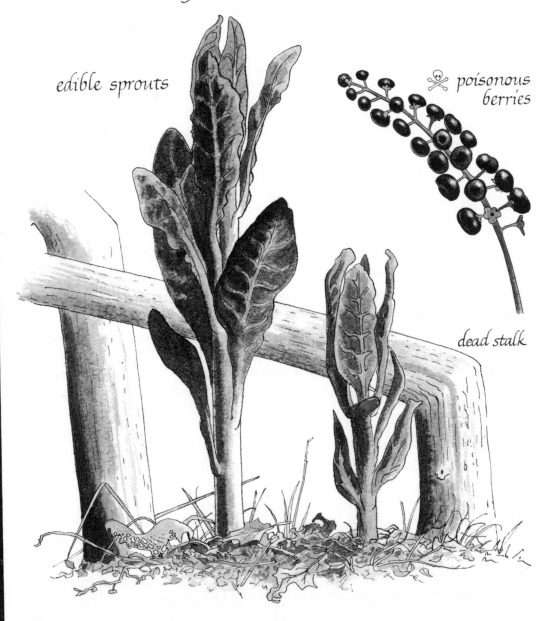

edible sprouts

☠ poisonous berries

dead stalk

You can extend the harvesting season by cutting off mature stalks, then waiting a few days for new sprouts to appear. To get rapid and maximum sprouting, cut all of the older stalks very close to the ground. Be sure to sever them completely. If they're attached by just a little tissue they manage to stay alive.

RECIPES

Poke sprouts can be used in any recipe that calls for asparagus. They can also be pickled (see Having Wild Foods All Year), and are quite delicious either steamed or boiled (see Cooking Tips, page 166).

Poke Leaves

Young leaves cut from the sides and tops of poke sprouts can be cooked like spinach, though they require a longer cooking time. Rinse them off and put them in a small amount of boiling salted water for about 10 minutes, then drain. Put the leaves in a small amount of fresh water and let them simmer for about a half-hour. Add salt and butter while the greens simmer; if necessary, season again later when they are tender and ready to serve.

Poke Leaves with Bacon

While poke leaves are simmering (see above), fry a few slices of bacon until crisp. Drain the bacon on paper towels, and when it is cool, crumble it. Reserve the bacon fat. Add the cooked poke leaves to the skillet and saute them until most of the bacon fat is absorbed by the leaves. Serve the poke leaves with bacon sprinkled on top.

Poke Casserole

INGREDIENTS

about 40 poke sprouts

4 eggs

2 tablespoons butter

1/4 cup flour

2 cups milk

1/2 cup finely chopped green pepper

1 teaspoon salt

1/4 teaspoon pepper

1/2 cup bread crumbs

EQUIPMENT

vegetable steamer

1 medium saucepan

bowlful of cold water

1 small saucepan

sharp knife

wire whisk

measuring cup

measuring spoons

2-quart baking dish

Yield: 4 to 6 servings

1. Wash the sprouts and remove leaves, except for small ones on tips. Steam or boil the sprouts until tender. Drain them thoroughly.
2. Put the eggs in a saucepan of boiling water, reduce heat to a simmer, cover the pan, and leave for 8 to 10 minutes. With a large spoon transfer the eggs to a bowl of cold water. Before they cool completely, crack their shells so they will peel more easily. When the eggs are cooled, peel and slice them.
3. Preheat the oven to 375° F.
4. Melt the butter in a small saucepan over moderate heat, then whisk in the flour.
5. Add the milk, then season with salt and pepper, stirring constantly.
6. Add the green pepper and let the sauce simmer for a few minutes.
7. Grease the bottom and sides of a 2-quart baking dish. Place about 10 poke sprouts on the bottom, pour some sauce over this, and then

top with several slices of egg. Continue making layers of poke, sauce, and egg slices.

8. Sprinkle the top with bread crumbs and bake in the preheated oven for 30 minutes.

Poke Omelet

INGREDIENTS	EQUIPMENT
4–6 poke sprouts	sharp knife
6 eggs at room temperature	small mixing bowl
3 teaspoons cold water	measuring spoons
1 tablespoon butter	frying pan or omelet pan
1/4 teaspoon paprika	spatula
salt* and pepper to taste	

* Salt tends to toughen eggs, so always add it just before serving.

Yield: 3 to 4 servings

1. Rinse the poke sprouts and cut them into half-inch pieces. Steam or boil them for about 10 minutes or until they are tender, then drain.

2. Break the eggs into a bowl, add the cold water, and beat with a fork for a few seconds, just until the yolks and whites are combined.

3. Heat a frying pan or omelet pan over a medium flame. Drop the butter in the pan. It should sizzle, but if the butter turns brown quickly, the pan is too hot. Spread the butter around by turning and tilting the pan.

4. Pour the eggs in and immediately add the cut-up pieces of poke. Swirl the eggs in a circular motion with the flat of a fork, or run a spatula around the edge to loosen the eggs and tilt the pan to allow the uncooked portion to run underneath.

5. When all of the egg mixture is cooked evenly, fold one edge over with the spatula and tilt the pan so that the omelet slides onto a heated serving plate. Add the seasonings.

Poke Sprouts on Toast

INGREDIENTS

about 20 poke sprouts

12 slices of bacon

2 tablespoons butter

2 tablespoons flour

1 cup milk

1/2 teaspoon salt

1/8 teaspoon pepper

3/4 cup coarsely grated
   cheddar cheese

4 slices bread

1 tablespoon chopped chives or
   fresh dill

EQUIPMENT

vegetable steamer

grater

frying pan

measuring cup

measuring spoons

medium saucepan

wire whisk

sharp knife

Yield: 4 servings

1. Wash the sprouts and snap off their leaves, except for the small ones at the tips. Steam or boil the sprouts until tender. Drain and keep warm.
2. Fry the bacon slowly until crisp, then drain it on paper towels.
3. In a saucepan over moderate heat melt the butter, then add the flour and stir until it is absorbed. Cook for a few seconds.
4. Whisk the milk, salt, and pepper into the sauce.
5. Continue stirring and cook the sauce for about 5 minutes. As it thickens, gradually stir in the cheese until it is thoroughly melted and mixed into the sauce.
6. Toast and butter 4 slices of bread.
7. On each of 4 plates place a piece of toast topped by 3 slices of bacon and several poke sprouts. Pour cheese sauce over all and sprinkle with chopped chives or dill. Serve immediately.

Cattail

❧ COMMON NAMES ❧

cat-o'-nine-tails, rushes, bulrushes

❧ SCIENTIFIC NAME ❧

Typha latifolia *(broad-leaved or common cattail) is the most widespread of four species in the United States.*

It is difficult to think of a plant that was more important to North American Indians, and sometimes to colonists from Europe. Cattail offers a lot of nutritious food all year long. According to a study by one botanist, an acre of cattails can yield 32 tons of flour. This is much greater than the yield of an acre of wheat or oats. Besides being a sort of wild-food smorgasbord, cattail has nonfood uses. Dried cattail leaves can be woven into baskets and chair seats, while fluffy cattail seeds have been used as stuffing for pillows and mattresses.

FINDING CATTAIL

❧ *Distribution.* Cattail species occur in all 50 states.
❧ *Habitat.* Cattail grows in wet places, such as marshes, ponds, and ditches, and at the edges of slow-moving streams.

Collecting the edible "cob" stage of cattail flower spikes.

RECOGNIZING CATTAIL

🌿 *Appearance.* Stemless, long-leaved plants that grow in dense clumps.

🌿 *Leaves.* An inch or less wide, up to six feet long, the simple leaves emerge from a tightly packed base in the wet ground or water.

🌿 *Flowers.* For a few weeks each summer the long flower stalk is topped with a double flower spike, one a bit above the other. At first the flower spikes are slender and green. The lower one is composed of female flowers. The top one is made up of male flowers; they drop golden pollen on the female flowers below, then wither away.

❧ *Fruit.* By midsummer the female flower spike has developed into a dark brown compact mass of seeds. It looks like a six-inch-long sausage or cigar. In the winter these seed masses break apart and look like blobs of fluff.

CAUTION

Avoid *Phragmites communis,* sometimes called reed grass, feathergrass, Carrizo, or foxtail reed. It is not poisonous; in fact, it is edible but has much less food value than cattail, with which it is sometimes confused. The stalks of *Phragmites* are cylindrical but smaller then those of cattail. Also, *Phragmites* grows to be nine to twelve feet tall, and is topped with a large plume of flowers which are first a light silvery-purple, then gray-gold.

HARVESTING CATTAIL

Usually cattails can be reached only by wading in shallow water, or walking on wet ground where your feet may sink in. So cattail harvesting usually means going barefoot or wearing boots or sneakers you don't mind getting wet.

In the spring watch for the swordlike new leaves. Take a firm grip on a few of the inner leaves and pull upward. The leaves will break free of the roots. Peel away more of the outer leaves in your hand, and you will get to a tender, bland-tasting white part, usually a few inches long. (Later in the summer this tender core is smaller.) It can be eaten raw in salads or cooked as a vegetable. It is sometimes called "Cossack asparagus" because Russians were so fond of this spring vegetable collected from cattail species that grow along the Don River.

A few weeks later, watch for the green flower spikes to de-

CATTAIL *Typha*

flower
spike   seeds

BLUE FLAG *(poisonous)*

rhizomes

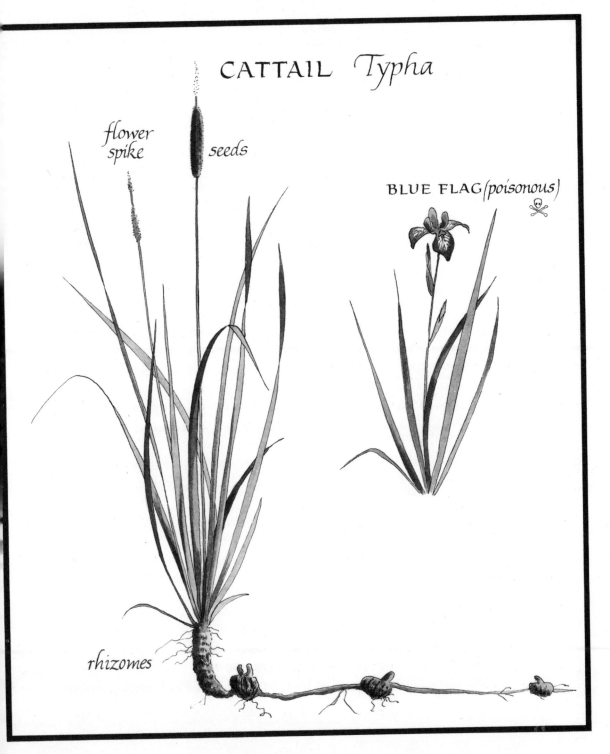

velop. At first they will be surrounded by a papery sheath like a corn husk. Don't bother with the most slender spikes on which the flowers have hardly developed; select only those from which you can easily scrape off some of the solid flower mass. Also don't collect those which are already covered with yellow pollen (the pollen is edible but it is not collected or prepared as spikes are), or which are beginning to turn brown.

Cut the spikes off with a knife or scissors, and leave about an inch of the stem on one end (for a handle when you eat the flowers later). All cattail flower spikes do not develop at once, so you will be able to harvest this food over a period of several weeks.

The yellow pollen can also be used as flour. Bend a cattail stem over so that its pollen-covered flower spike is directly above or inside a plastic bag or other container. Then shake the pollen off; if necessary, rub the remainder off with your fingers.

The underground part of the cattail is also edible and can be gathered year-round. You may need a shovel or spade, but if the soil is quite loose around the plant you may be able simply to reach down a few inches into the mud until you feel ropelike structures growing laterally. These are rhizomes — long underground stems. Grab a rhizome and pull up. You'll find that one cattail plant is connected to many others via a maze of rhizomes. They are edible, as are the bulblike sprouts that grow at the ends of rhizomes. Be sure to keep those underground parts moist (in a tightly sealed plastic bag) after you collect them; they're difficult to peel once they dry out.

CAUTION

Since some poisonous plants have underground bulbs, be sure that the rhizomes and bulblike parts you collect are attached to aboveground parts that are clearly cattails.

When collecting Cossack asparagus be sure that the cluster of young leaf shoots is cylindrical at its base. Blue flag, a poisonous species of wild iris, resembles young cattail in its early stages, but has clusters of young leaf stalks that are flattened at the base. Its rhizomes also have a strong, unpleasant taste, while cattail rhizomes are bland tasting.

RECIPES

Cattail rhizomes are often used as a source of cattail flour, produced by a rather laborious process described in detail by Euell Gibbons in his book *Stalking the Wild Asparagus.* Washed and peeled, cattail rhizomes can also be boiled and used as potato substitutes.

Cattail-on-the-Cob

Cattail flower spikes taste something like sweet corn, although they have a different texture. In most areas they are ready for harvest several weeks before fresh sweet corn, so they are one of the most popular of all wild foods.

Remove any husks. Drop the flower spikes into a pot of boiling, salted water, turn off the heat, cover the pot, and leave them for about 5 minutes. Then drain and serve the spikes. They can also be cooked in a vegetable steamer or fried in butter. Always serve them hot. The cooked flowers are rather dry, so spread them generously with butter and add salt. If you have fairly mature spikes, the masses of tiny flowers can easily be chewed off the tough, inedible "cob."

If you like the cornlike flavor of cattail flowers, try substituting cattail pollen for half of the flour required in recipes for pancakes, muffins, bread, and other baked goods.

Cattail-Pollen Pancakes

INGREDIENTS	EQUIPMENT
1 cup cattail pollen	fine-mesh sieve
1 cup unbleached white flour	flour sifter
3 teaspoons baking powder	large mixing bowl
1 teaspoon salt	measuring cup
1 tablespoon sugar	measuring spoons
2 eggs	small mixing bowl
1 1/2 cups milk	eggbeater or electric mixer
2 tablespoons melted butter or margarine	small saucepan
1/2 teaspoon cooking oil	frying pan or griddle
butter	spatula
maple syrup	

Yield: 4 servings

1. Put the pollen through a sieve to remove any debris.
2. Into a large bowl sift the pollen, flour, baking powder, salt, and sugar. With a spoon make a well in the center of the mixture.
3. In a small mixing bowl, beat the eggs lightly. Then pour them and the milk into the well in the flour.
4. Mix thoroughly; then add the melted butter and blend some more.
5. Heat a frying pan or griddle until a drop of water falling on its surface evaporates instantly. Grease the pan or griddle lightly with cooking oil.
6. Pour some pancake batter onto the surface and cook for 2 to 3 minutes, until small bubbles form on the tops of the pancakes. Turn with a metal spatula and cook the other side for about a minute. Serve with butter and maple syrup.

Golden Cattail Muffins

INGREDIENTS

1 cup cattail pollen

1 cup whole-wheat flour

2 teaspoons baking powder

1/2 teaspoon salt

1 egg

1/4 cup cooking oil

1/3 cup honey

1 1/2 cups milk

EQUIPMENT

muffin tins

18 paper muffin cups

fine-mesh sieve

flour sifter

measuring cup

measuring spoons

large mixing bowl

small mixing bowl

eggbeater or electric mixer

Yield: 18 muffins

1. Line the muffin tins with the paper muffin cups which have been greased lightly with oil.
2. Preheat the oven to 400° F.
3. Put the pollen through the sieve to remove any debris. Then sift it into a large bowl along with the flour, baking powder, and salt.
4. In small mixing bowl, beat the egg lightly. Add the oil, honey, and milk. Mix thoroughly.
5. Pour this mixture into the dry ingredients and stir for about half a minute. Then pour this mixture into the muffin cups, filling each about half to two-thirds full.
6. Bake in preheated oven for about 20 minutes. Serve with jam or honey.

Wild Strawberry

COMMON NAMES

Virginia strawberry, scarlet strawberry, wood strawberry, heartberry

SCIENTIFIC NAMES

There are several species, all in the genus Fragaria.

Commercially grown strawberries are big and beautiful, but usually have only a hint of the flavor of their smaller wild ancestors. Both the berries and the leaves are rich in vitamins A and C.

FINDING WILD STRAWBERRY

Distribution. Wild strawberry species grow throughout the original 48 states and in both Alaska and Hawaii.

Habitat. Wild strawberries are generally found in open weedy fields, on roadsides, and at the edges of woodlands.

Note the location where you find a wild strawberry patch
in flower; the fruit will be ripening about a month later.

RECOGNIZING WILD STRAWBERRY

Appearance. Low, creeping plants that spread by seeds and runners, which reach out from a parent plant, take root, and establish
new plants. Strawberries form an almost-solid ground cover in some
fields, though such taller plants as goldenrod often use the space above
them.

Leaves. Palmately compound, the three-toothed leaflets grow from a long, slightly hairy stalk.

Flowers. Several flowers, each with five white petals, grow at the end of a stalk covered with fine hairs.

Fruit. The true fruits are the tiny seeds on the outer surface of the bright red berries, which lie close to the ground.

HARVESTING WILD STRAWBERRY

Be alert for the ripening of these berries, which occurs in early summer in many states but may be earlier or later in some. Wild strawberries are often so well hidden under leaves that their two-to-three week season slips by without notice. In some years and in some places, wild strawberries are discouragingly tiny and scarce, so it is wise to explore several fields and other sites to try to find a place where they are bigger and more plentiful. Where wild strawberries are abundant, you can kneel in one spot, push aside some leaves, and find surprising numbers within easy reach. Wear long pants because strawberries sometimes grow among thorny plants and poison ivy.

Each berry is capped with tiny leaflike parts where it attaches to the stem. This cap is called the hull, and you should separate the hulls from the berries as you pick them, rather than later. Do this by holding the berry gently between two fingers of your "picking hand" and pinching the hull off with two fingers of the other hand. With practice you can do this without squashing the berry, even if your fingernails are short.

You needn't pick only deep-red and fully ripe berries. You can also pick light-red ones, and add a little more sugar or honey than recipes call for to compensate for their tartness. Even though you may be picking strawberries to use later in making a pie or some jam, be sure to make Instant Jam occasionally by popping some berries in your mouth, chewing slowly, and swallowing.

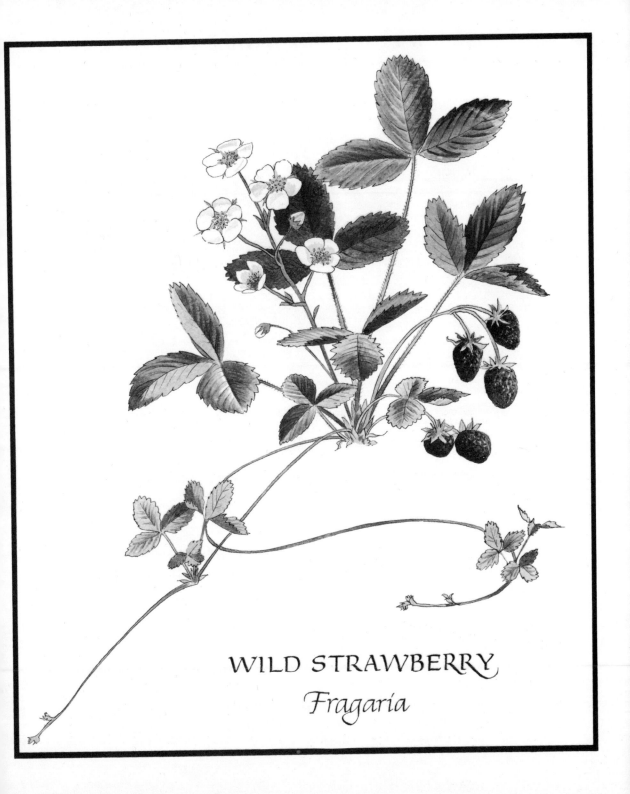

WILD STRAWBERRY

Fragaria

Delicious but small, wild strawberries are often overlooked.

RECIPES

Wild strawberries can be used in any recipe that calls for strawberries. You can also simply rinse the strawberries and serve them on ice cream, with cereal and milk, with cream and sugar, or mixed with yogurt.

Wild-Strawberry Tea*

Collect about 2 cups of strawberry leaves, wash them, and drop them into a saucepan containing a quart of boiling water. Turn off the heat and let the leaves steep in the water for about 5 minutes. Pour the liquid through a sieve or colander to remove the leaves, then serve the tea with a bit of lemon juice. Sweeten with honey or sugar if you like.

*Most teas are a blend of different kinds of leaves; the flavor of this tea will be improved if you add mint and raspberry leaves.

Wild-Strawberry Uncooked Jam*

INGREDIENTS

4 cups crushed wild strawberries

4 cups sugar

4 tablespoons lemon juice

1 bottle (6 fluid ounces) fruit
   pectin

EQUIPMENT

6–8 jars with tight-fitting lids

large mixing bowl

potato masher or wooden spoon

measuring cup

measuring spoons

small mixing bowl

Yield: about 8 cups of jam

1. Thoroughly wash several small jars and their lids, and have them ready for the jam.

2. Wash the berries, put them in a large bowl, and crush them with a potato masher or a wooden spoon. Measure to be sure you have 4 cups of crushed fruit.

3. Add the sugar to the berries, mix together thoroughly, and let stand for 10 minutes.

4. In another bowl mix the lemon juice and pectin, then add this to the fruit. Stir the mixture for 3 minutes.

5. Quickly pour the jam into the jars. Fill to within a half-inch of the top, then put the lid on tightly. (The goal is to expose the jam as little as possible to bacteria.)

6. Let the jam set at room temperature for about 24 hours. From then on, store in the freezer or refrigerator. Since it hasn't been cooked or put in sterilized jars, it cannot be stored in cupboards.

*This yields about 8 cups of jam, which will fill 6 to 8 small jars. The recipe can be halved. Also, packages or bottles of commercial pectin usually have recipes for jams and jellies, but these recipes call for what seems like an awful lot of sugar—perhaps because the manufacturers are also in the sugar business. You can experiment, using even less sugar than the amount suggested in this recipe. Remember, the less sweetening you use, the more the fruit flavor comes through in jams, pies, and other such treats.

Strawberry Chiffon Pie
with Graham Cracker Crust

INGREDIENTS FOR PIE CRUST

18 graham crackers

1/4 cup sugar

1/2 cup melted butter or margarine

EQUIPMENT FOR PIE CRUST

waxed paper

rolling pin

small mixing bowl

measuring cup

small saucepan

9-inch pie plate

8-inch pie plate (optional)

Yield: one 9-inch pie

1. Preheat the oven to 375° F.

2. Put the graham crackers on a sheet of waxed paper and then crush them with a rolling pin. They should yield about 1 2/3 cups of crumbs.

3. Put the crumbs in a small bowl and add the sugar and melted butter. Mix well.

4. Pour the crumb mixture into a 9-inch pie plate. Spread the crumbs around evenly on the bottom and sides of the plate. Pressing an 8-inch pie plate into the larger plate helps make an even crust.

5. Bake in the preheated oven for 8 minutes, remove, and allow to cool.

INGREDIENTS FOR PIE FILLING

1 envelope (1 tablespoon)
   unflavored gelatin

1/2 cup boiling water

1 1/2 cups crushed wild
   strawberries

EQUIPMENT FOR PIE FILLING

small saucepan

measuring cup

measuring spoons

3 medium mixing bowls

eggbeater or electric mixer

INGREDIENTS FOR PIE FILLING

1 teaspoon lemon juice

1 pinch salt

1 cup heavy cream (1/2 cup
   is optional)

2 egg whites

1/4 cup sugar

1 cup uncrushed wild strawberries
   (optional)

1. Dissolve the gelatin in the boiling water. Make sure all of the granules dissolve. Let it cool.
2. In a medium mixing bowl combine the gelatin solution and the crushed berries. Mix in the lemon juice and salt, then put the mixture in the refrigerator.
3. In a medium bowl whip 1/2 cup of heavy cream until it forms soft peaks when you lift the beater out.
4. After the berry mixture has chilled for several minutes, stick a spoon into it and pull it out. When a little mound is left where the spoon was placed, fold the whipped cream into the berry mixture.
5. In another bowl beat 2 egg whites until they form soft peaks. Gradually add 1/4 cup sugar and beat for another few minutes, until stiff, shiny peaks form.
6. Fold the egg whites into the berry mixture and pour this into the crust.
7. Chill the pie in the refrigerator for about 2 hours until it is firm.
8. The pie is quite beautiful and delicious just as it is, but you can serve it topped with a layer of whipped cream (1/2 cup heavy cream, whipped until it forms soft peaks) and 1 cup of whole berries sprinkled on top.

Sheep Sorrel

❦ COMMON NAMES ❦

field sorrel, red sorrel, sourgrass, rabbit ears, sour dock

❦ SCIENTIFIC NAME ❦

Rumex acetosella

For centuries Europeans have valued this plant as a food. It was probably brought deliberately to North America. Its tart, lemonlike flavor comes from crystals of calcium oxalate. Large amounts of this compound can be poisonous, and it is this substance that makes rhubarb leaves dangerous to eat. However, rhubarb stalks and spinach and sorrel leaves contain small amounts of calcium oxalate and millions of people eat these foods without ill effects. Also, much of this compound is destroyed when food is boiled or cooked—as it normally is when people eat fairly large amounts of sheep sorrel. During the 1970s, sorrel became increasingly popular among gourmet cooks in Europe and the United States.

The word "sorrel" comes from a German word meaning "sour," and there are other tart-tasting plants called sorrels which are not closely related to sheep sorrel. About thirty kinds of wood sorrel

Look for lush growths of sorrel leaves which can be
picked by the handful.

(of the genus *Oxalis*) grow in North America. All are rather delicate
plants with cloverlike leaves, which usually grow in moist woods. In
areas where wood sorrel is plentiful, it can be substituted for sheep
sorrel in recipes, though it tastes less tart than sheep sorrel.

FINDING SHEEP SORREL

彎 *Distribution.* Sheep sorrel grows in the original 48 states and in Alaska.

彎 *Habitat.* Sheep sorrel grows in open, dry areas such as fields or lawns, along roadsides, and along the edges of gardens where the soil is acid.

RECOGNIZING SHEEP SORREL

彎 *Appearance.* Low-growing plants with distinctive small leaves.

彎 *Leaves.* Up to about two inches long, the pale-green leaves are shaped like three-lobed arrowheads, or like the medieval weapons called halberds.

彎 *Flowers.* Tiny red flowers develop on the upper branches of the slender stem.

彎 *Fruit.* Tiny triangular brown seeds develop from the flowers.

彎 *Stems.* Up to a foot tall, the slender stem is topped with the inconspicuous flowers and no leaves.

HARVESTING SHEEP SORREL

Sheep sorrel is available for several months, from mid-spring to early autumn. Even though it is widespread and plentiful, you may have to search a bit to find many leaves of good flavor. Sometimes sheep sorrel grows in dense patches marked by their spindly reddish flower stalks. On these plants the leaves will be small, few in number, and rather bitter-tasting. Look in the vicinity and you may find sorrel plants that are not in flower. They may have scores of leaves up to two inches long, which have a delightful lemon flavor and which can be picked by the handful and brought home in plastic bags.

flowers

WOOD SORREL

SHEEP SORREL *Rumex acetosella*

RECIPES

A few sheep-sorrel leaves add a special tang to other greens in a salad. They are also good steamed, added to stews and soups, or used as seasoning for meat, fish, or potatoes.

Cream of Sorrel Soup

INGREDIENTS	EQUIPMENT
about 5 cups of sheep-sorrel leaves, chopped	sharp knife
1/4 cup butter	large stainless-steel or enamel saucepan*
1/2 cup chopped onion	measuring cup
3 cups fresh or canned chicken broth	measuring spoons
2 large egg yolks	small mixing bowl
1 cup heavy cream	eggbeater or electric mixer
1/8 teaspoon Tabasco sauce	wire whisk
salt and pepper to taste	

*Since sorrel is mildly acidic, cook it in stainless-steel or enamel pans. Do not cook in an aluminum pan to avoid discoloring the pan and adding a metallic taste to the cooked food.

Yield: 6 servings

1. Wash the sorrel leaves and remove most of the larger stems. Chop the leaves finely; you should have about 5 cups.
2. Melt the butter in a saucepan over medium heat, and then add the onion. Stir and cook until the onion is wilted.
3. Add the sorrel and continue to cook for a few minutes, until it is wilted.
4. Pour in the chicken broth and bring the mixture to a boil. Reduce the heat and let it simmer.

5. In a small bowl, beat the egg yolks. Add the cream, then a little of the hot broth to warm the mixture.

6. Stirring rapidly with a wire whisk, add the egg-cream mixture to the soup. Turn up the heat, but *don't let the soup boil.*

7. Add Tabasco sauce, salt, and pepper. The soup can be served hot or chilled.

Sheep-Sorrel Salad Dressing

INGREDIENTS	EQUIPMENT
1 cup sheep-sorrel leaves	sharp knife
3/4 cup water	small stainless-steel or enamel
1/2 cup sour cream	saucepan
1 teaspoon sugar	measuring cup
1/8 teaspoon salt	measuring spoons
1/8 teaspoon pepper	salad-dressing bottle or
	similar-sized jar with a lid

Yield: 1 cup of dressing

1. Wash the leaves, remove large stems, and chop the leaves finely.

2. In a small stainless-steel or enamel saucepan boil the water, add the sorrel, and cook over moderate heat for 5 minutes. Remove from the heat and let the leaves steep in the liquid for about 2 hours.

3. Drain and discard the leaves, reserving the sorrel liquid.

4. Pour 2 tablespoons of the sorrel liquid into a bottle or jar. Then add the sour cream, sugar, salt, and pepper.

5. Chill the dressing before use. It can be kept in the refrigerator for several weeks without spoiling. This tart dressing can take the place of lemon juice or vinegar on salads, fish, and other foods.

Sorrelade

For a lemonadelike beverage, simmer 2 to 3 cups of washed, chopped sorrel leaves in 5 to 6 quarts of water for about 20 minutes. Let the leaves steep in the water as it cools. Strain the liquid through a sieve or colander. Sweeten with honey or sugar if you like.

Sheep-Sorrel Pie

INGREDIENTS	EQUIPMENT
4 cups sheep-sorrel leaves	sharp knife
2 cups water	measuring cup
7 eggs, separated	measuring spoons
3/4 cup sugar	large stainless-steel or
1 homemade or store-bought	enamel saucepan
single-crust pastry for a 9-inch pie	small mixing bowl
	eggbeater or electric mixer
	small stainless-steel or
	enamel saucepan
	colander or sieve
	large mixing bowl

Yield: one 9-inch pie

1. Wash the sorrel leaves, remove the larger stems, and chop the leaves into fine pieces.

2. Put the water in a large stainless-steel or enamel saucepan and bring it to a boil. Add the sorrel and boil for 3 minutes. Remove from the heat and let the leaves steep in the liquid for a half-hour or more.

3. Preheat the oven to 400° F.

4. In a small mixing bowl beat the egg yolks for a minute. Gradually add 1/2 cup of sugar and keep beating—about 7 to 10 minutes—until the mixture is thick, heavy, and pale yellow in color.

5. Drain the sorrel, reserving the liquid. Discard the leaves. Add 1/2 cup of the liquid to the egg yolks and mix it in.

6. Put this mixture in a small stainless-steel saucepan and cook over low heat for about 5 minutes, stirring constantly with a wooden spoon. The mixture will thicken further. (Be sure to stir constantly or the mixture will burn.) Remove from the heat and let cool slightly.

7. In a large mixing bowl beat the egg whites until they are frothy. Slowly add the remaining 1/4 cup of sugar, and keep beating until the egg whites form stiff, shiny peaks.

8. Mix about a third of the egg whites into the egg yolks, then gently fold in the rest. Let this pie filling cool at room temperature.

9. As gently as possible pour the filling into the pie shell. Bake in the preheated oven for about 30 minutes or until the filling is lightly browned on top.

10. Cool at room temperature and then serve.

Watercress

❧ COMMON NAMES ❧

pepperleaf, water nasturtium

❧ SCIENTIFIC NAME ❧

Nasturtium officinale

Watercress is a wild plant that was and still is cultivated for food, and has "gone wild" again, although it is seldom found far from where people live. It is a member of the mustard family, and has the pungent taste of this group of plants. In fact its scientific name—*Nasturtium*—means "nose twister." Watercress is not related to the garden flower commonly called nasturtium, although it, too, has a pungent "nose twister" flavor.

FINDING WATERCRESS

❧ *Distribution.* Watercress occurs in all 50 states.
❧ *Habitat.* Look for watercress in the shallow, usually flowing cool water of brooks, springs, and ditches.

Small white flowers grow at the tips of watercress stems.

RECOGNIZING WATERCRESS

❧ *Appearance.* A floating or creeping plant with many small leaves, watercress sometimes grows in a thick mat, covering the surface of a small stream. But it isn't always directly in water, sometimes growing along stream edges, and also surviving on a mud flat if a stream dries up somewhat.

❧ *Leaves.* Pinnately compound, with three to eleven dark-green oval leaflets. The tip-end leaflet is the biggest. Leaflet edges are smooth but irregular.

❧ *Flowers.* Small, white, and four-petaled, watercress flowers grow at the stem tips.

❧ *Fruit.* Tiny seeds develop inside inch-long green pods.

❧ *Stems.* Up to several feet long, the flexible stems bear white threadlike roots at their joints.

White roots grow at intervals along the stems of watercress.

HARVESTING WATERCRESS

Watercress is available almost year-round in many areas. In winter, you can find watercress living in chilly water surrounded by ice and snow in some streams and springs. Pinch off leaflets and tender new stems and put them in a plastic bag. Watercress is easily transplanted to new streams, simply by pulling up a few stems with their little white roots, keeping them moist, and dropping them into the shallow waters of a new home.

CAUTION

If you have any doubts about the purity of the water in which the plants grow, reread the advice on pages 8–9.

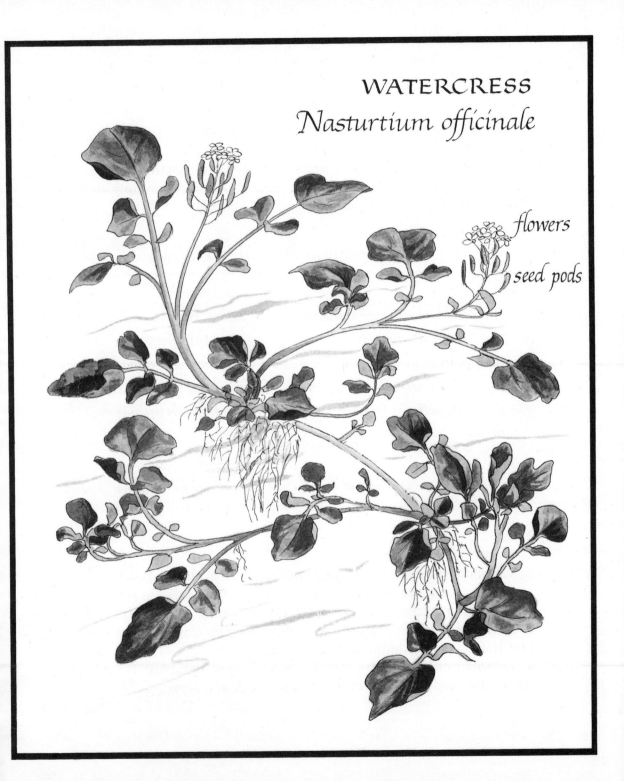

WATERCRESS
Nasturtium officinale

flowers

seed pods

RECIPES

After washing (and soaking in salted water to drive out snails and other aquatic animals), watercress can be eaten raw in salads. Use it instead of lettuce in a bacon, lettuce, and tomato sandwich or in other kinds of sandwiches. Here are five recipes including two for watercress soup, one simple, the other more complex.

*Watercress and Scrambled Eggs**

INGREDIENTS	EQUIPMENT
1 cup washed and drained watercress	sharp knife
4 eggs at room temperature	measuring cup
4 tablespoons cold water	measuring spoons
2 tablespoons butter or margarine	medium mixing bowl
1/2 teaspoon salt	medium frying pan
1 tablespoon chopped chives	fork
(optional)	spatula

*Watercress can also be used in the omelet recipe given for dandelion, page 40.

Yield: 2 to 4 servings

1. Chop the watercress.
2. Combine the eggs, water, and watercress in a mixing bowl.
3. Heat a frying pan to the point that the butter sizzles as it melts in the pan. Pour in the egg mixture. Stir with a fork, pulling the eggs in from the edges of the pan while tilting the pan from side to side so that the uncooked liquid goes to the edges.
4. Do this until the entire mixture is no longer liquid but is still soft and moist. Add salt, and chives, if you want, and serve.

Fancy Watercress Soup

INGREDIENTS

2 cups watercress

2 tablespoons butter

1 medium onion, finely chopped

1 bay leaf

2 medium potatoes, scrubbed,
  peeled, and diced

1 quart canned chicken broth
  (single strength)

1/2 teaspoon salt

1/8 teaspoon pepper

1 egg yolk

1/4 cup heavy cream

watercress leaves for garnish

EQUIPMENT

sharp knife

vegetable peeler

measuring cup

measuring spoons

large saucepan

small mixing bowl

eggbeater or electric mixer

Yield: 4 to 6 servings

1. Chop the washed and drained watercress.

2. In a large saucepan melt the butter, then add the watercress, onion, and bay leaf.

3. Sauté until the watercress is thoroughly wilted.

4. Add the potatoes, broth, salt, and pepper. Cook over moderate heat for 20 minutes.

5. Beat the egg yolk and cream together in a mixing bowl. Add a cup of hot soup to them, mix well, and then pour this into the soup.

6. Heat until warmed through *but do not boil*. Pour the soup into serving bowls, and garnish with uncooked watercress leaves.

Easy Watercress Soup

INGREDIENTS	EQUIPMENT
2 tablespoons flour	sharp knife
3 cups milk	measuring cup
1 tablespoon minced onion	measuring spoons
1/2 teaspoon salt	medium saucepan
2 cups finely chopped washed and drained watercress	wire whisk

Yield: 4 servings

1. In a medium saucepan, using a wire whisk, mix together the flour and 2 tablespoons milk.

2. Over moderate heat, slowly add the rest of the milk, the onion, and the salt.

3. Stir constantly as the mixture cooks. After it begins to boil and has thickened a bit, remove it from the heat and stir in the watercress. Serve immediately.

Stir-Fried Watercress

INGREDIENTS	EQUIPMENT
2 tablespoons cooking oil	large frying pan or wok
1 tablespoon grated fresh ginger root	measuring cup
	measuring spoons
10 cups washed and drained watercress	grater
	wooden spoon
1 tablespoon dark soy sauce	

Yield: 4 to 6 servings
1. In the frying pan or wok heat the oil until a drop of water added to it sizzles.
2. Add the grated ginger root to the hot oil, mix it in for a half-minute, then add the watercress.
3. Cook and stir with a wooden spoon for about 4 minutes. Then remove from the heat.
4. Add the soy sauce, mix it in thoroughly, and serve at once.

Watercress Salad Dressing

INGREDIENTS	EQUIPMENT
1/3 cup washed and drained	sharp knife
watercress	measuring cup
1 clove garlic, peeled	measuring spoons
1 1/2 cups olive oil	fork
1/2 cup wine vinegar or lemon juice	salad-dressing bottle or jar
salt and pepper to taste	with a lid
1 hard-boiled egg, peeled and	
finely chopped	

Yield: 2 cups of dressing
1. Finely chop the watercress.
2. Crush the garlic clove with the tines of a fork.
3. Add the garlic to the olive oil and vinegar or lemon juice in a jar or salad-dressing bottle.
4. Season with salt and pepper, and shake well to combine all ingredients.
5. Add the watercress and egg.
6. Store in the refrigerator and shake well before using.

Elderberry

blueberried elder, sweet elder, blackbead elder, American elderberry

The most common of several species are Sambucus canadensis *in the East and* Sambucus melanocarpa *in the West.*

Tests show that elderberries are a good source of calcium, iron, potassium, and vitamins A and C. Indians called the elderberry the "tree of music" because they made whistles, flutes, and other wind instruments from the stems. Elderberry is "musical" simply because its stems are easily hollowed out. You can poke out the soft pith with a stiff wire, then cut notches for different musical notes. Be sure to get all the pith out, since it is mildly poisonous.

Myths and superstitions surround the elderberry. In colonial New England many people planted an elderberry bush near their homes in the belief that it would protect them from witches.

The flat-topped clusters of elderberry flowers can be
snapped off with your fingers, and collected in a bag.

FINDING ELDERBERRY

🌿 *Distribution.* Elderberry species grow in all or nearly all of the
original 48 states and in Alaska.

🌿 *Habitat.* Elderberry shrubs usually grow in moist soil along roads,
in fields, and near ponds, marshes, and streams.

RECOGNIZING ELDERBERRY

❧ *Appearance.* A tall shrub with several branched stems and distinctive large white flower clusters.

❧ *Leaves.* The leaves grow opposite one another and are pinnately compound, with five to eleven leaflets which have pointed tips and finely toothed edges.

❧ *Flowers.* Small star-shaped white flowers grow in flat-topped clusters (cymes), some bigger than saucers.

❧ *Fruit.* Three tiny seeds develop within each deep purple or black berry. The stems bend over with the weight of the berry clusters.

❧ *Stems.* Young stems have greenish bark and a large core of soft white pith; older stems, up to twelve feet tall, have grayish-brown bark and a smaller core of soft brown pith.

CAUTION

Several kinds of shrubs have white flower clusters, but they are not shaped like those of elderberry, nor do they have the elderberry's distinctive leaves and pithy stems.

The fruit of red elderberries (*Sambucus pubens*, *Sambucus racemosa*, and other species) make some people ill. The ripe fruit of these shrubs is red, not dark blue. Also, the flower and berry clusters of red elderberries are rounded, not flat like those of the blueberried elder.

HARVESTING ELDERBERRY

The flower clusters, called elderblow, can be gathered in early summer when they are fully opened. Don't take older ones whose petals are beginning to turn brown at the edges. You can cut the stems or break them easily with your fingers. The same applies to the dark berries—it is easy to gather several pounds from a few

ELDERBERRY *Sambucus*

pith in stem

AMERICAN

INEDIBLE
*flower and fruit clusters
of Red Elderberry*

EDIBLE
*flower and fruit clusters
of American Elderberry*

bushes simply by snapping off the stems of berry clusters and dropping them into a large plastic bag or other container.

Most foragers prefer the flavor of dried berries to fresh ones.
Strip the berries from their stems and spread them on newspapers or
trays in the sun or in a warm room for several days. They can also be
placed on cookie sheets and dried in a 140° F oven (with the door
slightly open to allow water vapor to escape). Store them in tightly
sealed jars or plastic bags.

Some people get upset stomachs from eating many uncooked
berries from the blueberried elder. If you want to sample them, try
just a few. You may not like their taste anyway, but don't give up on
elderberries. They are one fruit that tastes much better when dried
and then prepared in pies, pancakes, and so on.

RECIPES

Elderberry Apple Pie

INGREDIENTS	EQUIPMENT
3 cups elderberries	small mixing bowl
3 cups peeled, cored, and sliced apples	large mixing bowl
3 tablespoons flour	paring knife
1 cup sugar	grater
1/2 teaspoon mace	measuring cup
1/2 teaspoon grated lemon rind	measuring spoons
1 homemade or store-bought double-crust pastry for a 9-inch pie	9-inch pie plate
2 tablespoons butter	

Yield: one 9-inch pie

1. For best results, use dried elderberries. Soak them for a half-hour in a bowl with a little water.

2. Preheat the oven to 450° F.

3. Put three cups of the berries and their juice in a large bowl. Then add the apples, flour, sugar, mace, and lemon rind.

4. Mix thoroughly and then pour into the pastry-lined pie plate.

5. Dot the pie filling with butter and cover with the remaining pastry. Squeeze the edges of the top and bottom crusts together with your fingers, then use the tines of a fork to press all around the edge, making a tight seal.

6. Bake the pie in preheated oven for 10 minutes. Then reduce the heat to 400° F and bake for an hour. Remove the pie from the oven when the crust is browned. The pie is best served warm. Try it with ice cream.

Deep-Fried Elderblow Fritters

INGREDIENTS

about 8–10 elderblow clusters

1 cup flour

1 teaspoon baking powder

1/4 teaspoon salt

2 eggs, separated

1/2 cup orange juice

about 2 cups cooking oil

EQUIPMENT

scissors (optional)

2 small mixing bowls

large mixing bowl

measuring cup

measuring spoons

eggbeater or electric mixer

large saucepan

deep-frying thermometer (optional)

spatula or slotted spoon

paper towels

Yield: 4 to 6 servings

1. The flowers can be left on their stems or separated with scissors.
2. In a large mixing bowl combine the flour, baking powder, and salt.
3. Beat the egg yolks slightly and add them to the flour mixture. Then add the juice and mix thoroughly.
4. In a small mixing bowl, beat the egg whites until they form soft peaks, then fold the whites into the batter. If you have de-stemmed the flowers, fold them in, too.
5. Put the oil in a large saucepan and heat it to about 375° F on a deep-frying thermometer. If you have no thermometer, just drop some batter into the oil to check its temperature. The batter should turn light brown in 3 to 4 minutes.
6. Drop tablespoonfuls of the flower batter into the hot oil, and let them fry until they are golden brown. Do not overcrowd the pan or the temperature of the oil will drop.
7. If you left the flowers on their stems, pick up each cluster by its stem, dip it into the batter, then drop into the oil and fry as described in step 6.
8. Remove the fritters with a spatula or slotted spoon, and drain on paper towels.
9. Sprinkle with confectioner's sugar, drops of honey, jam, or whipped cream, and serve while still warm.

Elderblow Pancakes

INGREDIENTS	EQUIPMENT
2 eggs	medium mixing bowl
2 tablespoons butter or margarine, softened to room temperature	wire whisk
	measuring cup
1 1/2 cups milk	measuring spoons

INGREDIENTS

2 cups flour

2 teaspoons baking powder

1 tablespoon honey or 2 tablespoons
  sugar

1/2 teaspoon salt

1 cup elderberry flowers, with
  stems removed

1 tablespoon cooking oil

EQUIPMENT

scissors

wooden spoon

frying pan or griddle

spatula

Yield: 4 to 6 servings

1. In a medium mixing bowl beat the eggs well, using a whisk. Then mix in the butter and milk.

2. Add the flour, baking powder, sugar or honey, salt, and finally the flowers. Blend using a wooden spoon.

3. Heat a frying pan or griddle. Grease it lightly with cooking oil.

4. For each pancake drop about 1/4 cup of the batter onto the pan, turning it over with the spatula when bubbles form on top. Cook only half as long on the second side.

5. Serve with maple syrup or jam.

Elderblow-Mint Tea

Put several clusters of elderberry flowers and some mint leaves (see page 110) in a few quarts of water and boil them for 10 minutes. Let them steep in the water as it cools. Strain out the flowers and mint. Add lemon juice and sweetening if you want.

Milkweed

❧ COMMON NAMES ❧

silkweed, common milkweed, cottonweed

❧ SCIENTIFIC NAMES ❧

Asclepias syriaca *and* Asclepias speciosa *are common
representatives of this group, which includes many native species.*

As you break off a stalk, leaf, or flower cluster, you can see how the plant gets its name: a milky sap flows out. In some milkweeds, the sap is bitter-tasting and can make animals ill. Monarch butterflies and other insects that feed on milkweed have some of this bitter-tasting chemical in their bodies. As a result, insect-eating birds learn to avoid the monarch and other milkweed-fed animals.

In midsummer watch for yellow, white, and black-striped caterpillars on milkweed plants. They are the larvae of monarch butterflies. You can raise one to be a butterfly if you have a steady supply of fresh milkweed leaves for it to eat. For a cage, use an empty aquarium with a top of cardboard, aluminum foil, or screening held in place with tape. You can also use window screening to make a simple cage, tying sections together with twine or lightweight wire. When the caterpillar is fully grown, about two inches long, it will form a light-green chrysalis. A monarch butterfly will emerge from the chrysalis about twelve to fifteen days later. When its wings are fully open and dry, let it fly away.

Each milkweed plant usually has several clusters of flowers.

FINDING MILKWEED

🌿 *Distribution.* Milkweed species occur in the original 48 states and in Alaska.

🌿 *Habitat.* Milkweed flourishes in weedy fields and along roadsides and fences.

RECOGNIZING MILKWEED

🌿 *Appearance.* Tall weeds with dull-green leaves, usually growing in clumps.

🌿 *Leaves.* Simple and tapered at both ends, the leaves of the most common broad-leaved species are from four to eight inches long and grow opposite one another. Their undersides are light-colored and coated with fine hairs.

🌿 *Flowers.* With five petals, the fragrant pink to purple flowers are arranged in clusters called umbels.

Milkweed seed pods make a delicious vegetable if you
harvest them before the seeds inside are fully developed.

🌿 *Fruit.* Small dark brown seeds, each with a white silk streamer,
develop within dull green pods, two to five inches long, which have a
bumpy outer surface.

🌿 *Stems.* These are sturdy and unbranched, usually three to four
feet tall, and covered with fine hairs.

CAUTION

In the West some kinds of narrow-leaved milkweed are poisonous to livestock and shouldn't be eaten. Except for their milky
sap they do not resemble the common milkweed shown here.

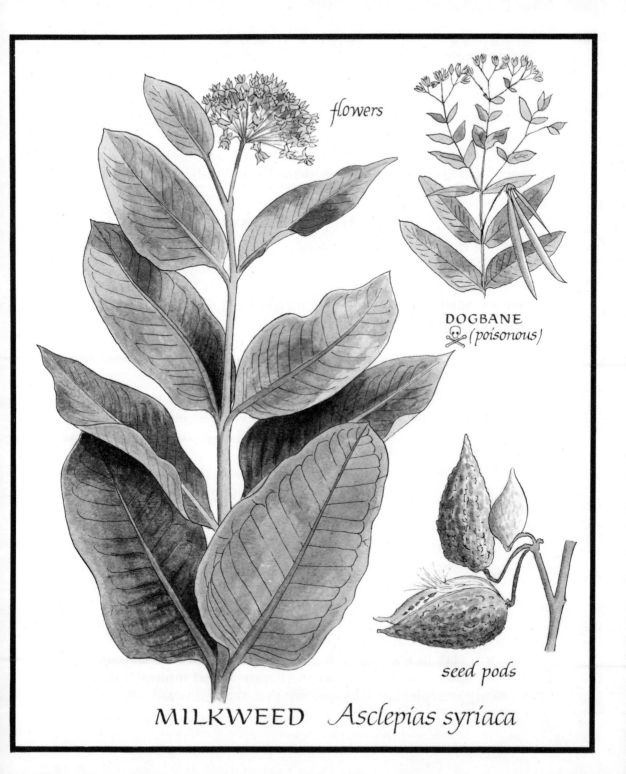

flowers

DOGBANE (poisonous)

seed pods

MILKWEED *Asclepias syriaca*

Dogbane is another poisonous plant with milky sap. It looks something like milkweed when both are in the young sprout stage, but in its mature stage, dogbane has no fine hairs on its leaves and stems. When mature, dogbane stems branch, and its flowers are bell-shaped and far fewer in number than those of milkweed.

HARVESTING MILKWEED

In the opinion of most foragers, the tastiest parts of the milkweed are the flower buds and seed pods. Cut clusters of green flower buds from the stems. Later on, you can snap off the seed pods when they are small (up to about two inches long) and fairly firm, before the silk streamers are fully formed inside.

RECIPES

Raw milkweed is usually considered inedible because of the taste of its sap and because it has made children ill, but proper cooking produces a safe and flavorsome vegetable. The treatment is the same for flower buds and seed pods.

Wash the milkweed and put it in a saucepan. In a separate pan heat to boiling about 3 quarts of water. Pour enough of this water on the milkweed to cover it, turn up the heat, and boil for about 2 minutes. Pour off this water, add fresh boiling water, and boil for about 2 minutes again. The third time you pour fresh boiling water on the milkweed, let it boil for about 5 minutes. Drain the milkweed in a colander, then serve. If you simply add butter and salt, you have a delicious dish.

Be sure that the water you add to the milkweed is very hot; if you put milkweed in cool water and then bring it to a boil the bitter taste will stay in the vegetable. The liquid you discard contains not only the bitter taste but also some vitamin C and minerals; this loss is usually unavoidable. Chances are that the milkweed will still be more nutritious than most store-bought produce.

The procedure described above is the traditional method for cooking milkweed. However, some foragers use only one boiling water bath for milkweed, and some use none at all. Some people eat raw milkweed flower buds and seed pods, and find them delicious. This is a matter of personal taste, and depends perhaps also on the species of milkweed used. Until more is known, let others explore this frontier of foraging.

Milkweed Omelet or Quiche

Once they have been treated to remove their bitter taste, the edible parts of milkweed, chopped, can be used instead of dandelion in the omelet recipe on page 40 or instead of lamb's-quarters in the quiche recipe on page 138. Use approximately the same amount.

Milkweed Casserole

INGREDIENTS

about 20 milkweed flower clusters

8 tablespoons butter or margarine

4 tablespoons flour

2 cups milk

1 cup grated sharp cheddar cheese

1 teaspoon salt

1/8 teaspoon pepper

1 cup bread crumbs

EQUIPMENT

medium saucepan

2-quart baking dish

measuring cup

measuring spoons

wire whisk

grater

small saucepan

Yield: 6 to 8 servings

1. First prepare the flower clusters as described above, to remove their bitter taste.

2. Grease the bottom and sides of the baking dish, and arrange the milkweed on the bottom.

3. Preheat the oven to 350° F.

4. Over low heat melt 4 tablespoons of butter in a medium saucepan, add the flour, and mix them thoroughly with a whisk.

5. Add the milk gradually, stirring constantly. Increase the heat and keep stirring until the mixture thickens.

6. Add the cheese, salt, and pepper. Mix well until the cheese melts. Taste to see if further seasoning is needed.

7. Pour the sauce over the milkweed.

8. In a small saucepan melt the remaining 4 tablespoons of butter and add the bread crumbs. Mix well, and sprinkle this mixture on top of the cheese sauce.

9. Bake in the preheated oven for about 20 minutes, or until the bread crumbs are browned.

Milkweed Seed-Pod Soup

INGREDIENTS	EQUIPMENT
about 6 cups milkweed seed pods	colander
2 beef bouillon cubes, dissolved	sharp knife
in 2 cups hot water	small saucepan
4 tablespoons butter	2 large saucepans
1/2 cup flour	measuring cup
1 egg yolk	measuring spoons

INGREDIENTS

1 cup light cream

1 teaspoon salt

1/4 teaspoon pepper

1/4 teaspoon lemon juice

EQUIPMENT

slotted spoon

wire whisk

small mixing bowl

Yield: 6 to 8 servings

1. Follow the above cooking procedure for milkweed, using boiling water baths. After the seed pods have been drained, cut them into 1/4-inch lengths.

2. Put the pods and bouillon in a large saucepan and bring to a boil. Reduce the heat and simmer for about 15 minutes. With a slotted spoon remove the pods and set them aside. Reserve the bouillon.

3. Melt butter in a large saucepan over low heat.

4. Add the flour and mix it in thoroughly.

5. Stir vigorously with a wire whisk as you add the reserved bouillon. Increase the heat and let the mixture come to a boil. Reduce the heat and simmer for about 5 minutes.

6. Add the milkweed pods and simmer for another 15 to 20 minutes.

7. Using a whisk, beat the egg yolk and cream together. Gradually add 1/2 cup of the hot soup to the egg yolk mixture. Then add this to the soup, a little at a time.

8. Add salt, pepper, and lemon juice. Heat the soup through *(do not let it boil)* and serve.

Wild Mint

🌿 COMMON NAMES 🌿

peppermint, spearmint, field mint, watermint

🌿 SCIENTIFIC NAMES 🌿

Mentha piperita *(peppermint)*, Mentha spicata *(spearmint), and*
Mentha arvensis *(Western mint) are common species.*

As garden plants, spearmint and peppermint were brought to North America from Europe. Many acres of them are grown to provide mint for commercial products. They also grow wild. There are also several native kinds of mint, each with a distinctive odor and taste. All mints are rich in vitamins A and C.

FINDING WILD MINT

🌿 *Distribution.* Wild mint species grow in all 50 states.
🌿 *Habitat.* Mint grows best in wet places in meadows, fields, and ditches and along the sides of streams.

Wild mint often grows in sunny places at the edge of a stream.

RECOGNIZING WILD MINT

❧ *Appearance.* Dark-green plants that often grow in clumps in wet places.

❧ *Leaves.* Growing opposite one another, the dark-green leaves are deeply veined. Peppermint leaves are evenly toothed. Spearmint leaves are unevenly toothed. Smell and taste are clues to telling these two mints apart. Peppermint leaves have a strong menthol taste, while spearmint leaves have the familiar taste of mint candy, gum, tea, and jelly. However, even the taste of spearmint varies widely.

❧ *Flowers.* In spearmint, small pink-to-violet flowers grow where leaves are attached to the stem. Peppermint flowers grow on a short spike at the tops of stems.

❧ *Fruit.* The seeds are tiny and inconspicuous.

❧ *Stems.* Up to two feet tall, in cross section mint stems have four sides.

HARVESTING WILD MINT

Once you've found a clump of mint, you can simply pick the leaves one by one and collect them in a plastic bag. But first sample the leaves: crush them, smell them, taste them. You may find that smaller, young leaves are superior to bigger ones. Also, the "mint-iness" varies from one clump to another, so it may be worthwhile to search for another, more flavorful mint patch.

RECIPES

Mint is pleasant to nibble on, just as you pluck it. Chopped finely, it adds a special tang to a mixture of other greens in a salad. Mint also adds a nice flavor when used as a garnish on ice cream or sherbet. Leaves can be steamed or boiled for a few minutes and served as a cooked vegetable.

Wild Mint Salad Dressing

INGREDIENTS	EQUIPMENT
1 cup wine vinegar	small saucepan
4 tablespoons sugar	measuring cup
1/2 teaspoon salt	measuring spoons
dash of cayenne pepper	salad-dressing bottle or
4 tablespoons chopped fresh mint	jar with lid
leaves	

Yield: about 1 cup of dressing

1. In saucepan mix and heat the vinegar, sugar, salt, and cayenne. Bring to a boil, remove from heat, and pour immediately over the mint leaves in the bottle or jar.
2. Chill and store capped in the refrigerator. This dressing is especially delicious on sliced tomatoes or cucumbers.

flowers

flowers

PEPPERMINT
Mentha piperita

SPEARMINT
Mentha spicata

Mint Tea

INGREDIENTS	EQUIPMENT
1 quart water	medium saucepan or teakettle
2 1/2 tablespoons chopped fresh or	teapot
dry mint leaves	strainer
honey or sugar to taste	

Yield: 4 cups

1. Bring the water to a boil. Put the leaves in a teapot, pour the water over the leaves, and let steep for at least 5 minutes.
2. Pour through a strainer to remove the leaves, and serve.

Wild-Mint Jelly

INGREDIENTS	EQUIPMENT
2 cups fresh mint leaves	5–7 jelly jars with lids
1 apple	shallow pan
3 cups water	small saucepan
2 tablespoons lemon juice	sharp knife
2 1/2 cups sugar	paring knife
5 drops green food coloring	large stainless-steel or enamel
(optional)	saucepan
1/2 bottle fruit pectin (3 ounces)	sieve or strainer
paraffin	measuring cup
	measuring spoons
	metal spoon

Yield: about 5 small jars

In jelly making, the jelly, jars, and paraffin must all be ready simulta-

neously, so it is easier—and more fun—to share the work with at
least one other person. First prepare the jars or glasses so that they
will be sterile and ready for filling with jelly. After washing them
thoroughly, fill each about three-fourths full of water and set in a
shallow pan that is partly filled with water. Set the lids lightly on
the jars. Let the water simmer around and in the jars while you prepare the jelly. Shortly before the jelly is ready, take the jars from
their pan, empty them, and set them upside down on a drying rack to
drain. They should be dry but still hot when jelly is poured.

Melt the paraffin in a small saucepan over low heat. Just melt
it, don't let it get very hot. Have it ready to pour on top of the jelly
immediately after jelly is poured into a jar.

To make the jelly:
1. Wash the mint leaves, removing any that are bruised, discolored,
or wilted. Drain and chop into small pieces.
2. Peel and core the apple and cut into 8 pieces.
3. Put the apple and mint in a large stainless-steel or enamel saucepan and cover with water. Bring to a boil and cook for 5 minutes,
stirring occasionally. Remove from heat, cover, and let the mint
steep in the pan for about 10 minutes.
4. Strain the leaves from the liquid, reserving the liquid. Return
1 3/4 cups of this liquid to the same pan.
5. Add lemon juice, sugar, and food coloring. Stir frequently as you
bring this mixture to a boil. (The food coloring is optional; without it
the jelly is a transparent light-yellow color.)
6. Add the pectin, mix it in thoroughly, and then let the mixture
boil for one minute as you stir constantly. Remove from the heat and
skim off the foam with a spoon.
7. Pour the mint jelly immediately into the sterilized jars to within
1/4 inch of the top, then cover the surface quickly with about 1/8
inch of melted paraffin.
8. If the jars were sterilized and quickly and completely sealed, this
jelly can be stored in a cupboard for long periods without spoiling. It
needn't be refrigerated until after the paraffin seal is broken.

Wild Raspberries and Blackberries

❦ COMMON NAMES ❧

black raspberry, blackberry, red raspberry, wineberry, thimbleberry, cloudberry, dewberry, salmonberry, blackcap

❦ SCIENTIFIC NAMES ❧

All species are in the genus Rubus; *the scientific names of some of the most common species are given below.*

The genus *Rubus* gives botanists plenty of trouble, since there are more than 200 species in North America. Crossbreeding between species makes it even more difficult to tell one kind from another. Foreign varieties have also become established in North America, adding to the confusion about plant identity. Berry pickers often disagree about the name of what they're collecting, but they agree on the fine flavor. None of the species above grows nationwide, but every region has at least a few kinds of *Rubus* to search for.

Black raspberry — showing ripe fruit and lighter unripe fruit, as well as stalks from which fruit was picked.

FINDING WILD RASPBERRIES AND BLACKBERRIES

❦ *Distribution.* Wild raspberry species grow in all 50 states. Blackberries occur in the Northeast, south to Tennessee and North Caro-
lina, west to Minnesota and Indiana.

❦ *Habitat.* These grow best in overgrown fields and thickets, along
fences and the edges of forests, and on roadsides.

RECOGNIZING WILD RASPBERRIES AND BLACKBERRIES

❦ *Appearance.* There are many species, and a great range of characteristics, in the genus *Rubus*. Nearly all members of the genus have
white flowers, compound leaves, and prickly or bristly stems. They
grow in a vaselike form, with the stems (called canes) arching up,
then back toward the ground.

❦ *Leaves.* Red raspberry *(Rubus strigosus)* has pinnately compound
leaves with three to seven toothed leaflets that have whitish undersides. Brought from Asia to North America, wine raspberry or wine-

berry *(Rubus phoenicolasius)* has similar leaves, but its end leaflets are somewhat heart-shaped. Black raspberry or blackcap *(Rubus occidentalis)* has five leaflets in a fan-shaped group (palmately compound). Blackberry *(Rubus allegheniensis)* has three to seven leaflets (usually five), also arranged like an open fan.

✻ *Flowers.* Most species in the genus *Rubus* have similar five-petaled white flowers that develop in clusters on stems that are in their second year.

✻ *Fruit.* The berries are not true berries but a cluster of many tiny rounded pulpy fruits, each containing a small hard seed. The fruits of red raspberry are dull red; those of wine raspberry are shiny red and feel a little sticky; those of black raspberry are black. The cluster of fruits making up a raspberry is hollow—like a little cap—and fits onto a little white stalk, which is revealed when you pick one. The cluster of fruits making up a blackberry is not hollow and leaves no white stalk when picked.

✻ *Stems.* Red raspberry usually has round, bristly stems; wine raspberry has round stems covered with many reddish hairs; black raspberry has round stems with strong hooked bristles; blackberry usually has strong angular (not round) stems with stout prickles.

HARVESTING WILD RASPBERRIES AND BLACKBERRIES

Wild raspberries ripen in midsummer in many states (somewhat earlier in warmer climates, later in colder climates). Raspberry patches seem almost impenetrable at times, so wear long pants and a long-sleeved shirt for protection from scratches. Often the biggest berries develop in partly shaded places rather than in full sunlight.

Sometimes raspberry fruits are so plentiful that you can pick several at once. To do this, apply just enough pressure with your fingers to force the ripe fruits off their little stalks, but not enough to crush them. This technique works well because unripe fruits cling to their stalks, while you easily remove the ripe and nearly ripe ones.

RASPBERRIES and BLACKBERRIES *Rubus*

BLACKBERRY

RED
RASPBERRY

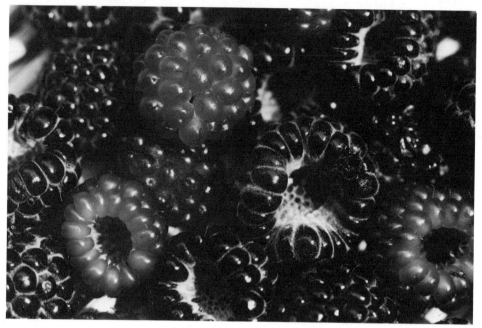

A closeup view of wineberries and black raspberries reveals their hollow, caplike form.

RECIPES

Like strawberries and blueberries, after a rinsing, these fruits can be eaten just as you pick them, on ice cream or cereal, in yogurt, or in a bowl with milk or cream.

Wild-Raspberry Uncooked Jam

Use the recipe for wild-strawberry jam (page 75). Experiment with the amount of sugar, since different varieties of raspberries vary somewhat in their natural sugar content.

Wild-Raspberry Bavarian Cream Pie

INGREDIENTS

2 cups wild raspberries or
  blackberries
1/2 cup sugar
1 1/2 teaspoons unflavored gelatin
3 tablespoons water
3 tablespoons boiling water
1/2 tablespoon lemon juice
1/2 cup heavy cream
1 homemade or store-bought
  single-crust pastry for a
  9-inch pie, prebaked

EQUIPMENT

wooden spoon
medium mixing bowl
2 small mixing bowls
measuring cup
measuring spoons
small saucepan
eggbeater or electric mixer
9-inch pie plate

Yield: one 9-inch pie

1. With a wooden spoon, crush the berries in a medium mixing bowl. Add the sugar, and let the mixture stand for half an hour.
2. In a small bowl, soak the gelatin in the water for a few minutes. Add the boiling water to dissolve the gelatin. (Be sure there are no crystals left.)
3. Stir the gelatin into the berries. Add the lemon juice.
4. Put the fruit-gelatin mixture in the refrigerator to set.
5. With an electric mixer or egg beater, whip the cream.
6. When the fruit-gelatin mixture becomes a bit firm (test with a spoon; it should leave a little mound on the surface when you pull the spoon out), fold in the whipped cream, then pour into the baked pie shell.
7. Refrigerate for at least 2 hours before serving. You can decorate the pie by placing whole raspberries around its outer edge.

Raspberry Cake

INGREDIENTS

10 tablespoons butter or margarine

4 eggs

1 cup sugar

1/2 cup sifted flour

1/2 cup cornstarch

1 teaspoon baking powder

2 1/2 cups wild raspberries*

EQUIPMENT

2 small mixing bowls

wire whisk or electric mixer

measuring cup

measuring spoons

flour sifter

9-inch round cake pan

*You can substitute blackberries, strawberries, or blueberries for the raspberries called for in the recipe.

Yield: 9-inch single-layer cake

1. Preheat the oven to 400° F.

2. In a small mixing bowl, cream the butter with an electric mixer, or by hand with a whisk, until it is soft and mushy.

3. In a separate small bowl break the eggs. Add the sugar and beat for at least 5 minutes, until the mixture is thick and pale yellow.

4. Add the creamed butter to the egg-sugar mixture and beat until fluffy, about 2 minutes.

5. Sift the flour, cornstarch, and baking powder together into a bowl. Then fold this mixture into the egg-sugar mixture. Add the fruit to the batter.

6. Generously grease the cake pan. Pour in the batter. Tap the pan on the counter to spread the batter evenly and to burst air bubbles.

7. Bake in the middle rack of the oven. Immediately reduce the temperature to 375° F and bake for 25 to 30 minutes, until the top is golden and the edges of the cake start to shrink away from the sides.

Glazed sugar topping: Place the cake on a Pyrex or other platter that can go into the oven. Sprinkle the top with sugar or honey. Place the cake under the broiler for 2 minutes. Again sprinkle with sugar or honey and place under the broiler for another minute. Watch carefully so as not to burn the cake.

*Raspberry Ices**

INGREDIENTS	EQUIPMENT
1 cup water	small saucepan
1/2 cup sugar	measuring cup
2 cups crushed wild raspberries or	measuring spoons
blackberries	ice-cube trays or a shallow dish
2 tablespoons lemon juice	

Yield: 4 to 6 servings

1. In a saucepan over moderate heat mix together the water and sugar. Heat to a full boil and boil for 5 minutes.
2. Add the raspberries and lemon juice.
3. Pour the mixture into ice-cube trays or a shallow dish and place in the freezer.
4. When the water becomes slushy, stir it to reduce the size of the ice crystals. Repeat at half-hour intervals until the mixture is all coarse ice crystals.
5. Put in the refrigerator about 15 minutes before serving.

*To make blueberry ices, follow the same recipe but use less lemon juice.

Daylily

❧ COMMON NAMES ❧

garden lily, tawny-orange lily, lemon lily

❧ SCIENTIFIC NAMES ❧

Hemerocallis fulva *(orange flowers)*, Hemerocallis flava *(yellow flowers)*

The daylily was brought deliberately from Europe as a garden plant. Unlike many garden flowers, however, it survives well without human care. It "escapes" easily, and a single plant can expand into a large clump in a few years. Daylilies multiply mostly by underground branches (rhizomes) that reach out from a cluster of food-storing parts called tubers. (The potatoes we eat are also tubers.) The blossoms open fully for just one day and then die; this is the origin of the plant's name.

Daylilies have three edible parts: the tubers, young leaf stalks, and the flower buds and flowers. The flower buds of the tiger lily, a rather distant relative of the daylily, are often used in Oriental cuisine. They are added to soups, meat dishes, and noodles, and can be bought (usually in dried form) in gourmet food shops and Oriental food stores, where they are called "golden needles." Daylily flowers can also be used in recipes calling for golden needles.

Daylily flowers and flower buds of all sizes are edible.

FINDING DAYLILY

🌿 *Distribution.* Daylily grows throughout most of the eastern United States, west to Minnesota and Texas.

🌿 *Habitat.* Daylily grows along roadsides, at the edges of fields, and in gardens (including abandoned gardens near old homesites).

RECOGNIZING DAYLILY

🌿 *Appearance.* Stemless, long-leaved plants with large orange or yellow flowers.

🌿 *Leaves.* From three to six feet long, narrow and pointed, daylily leaves arise directly from the ground.

❦ *Flowers.* Slender, round flower stalks, up to four feet tall, bear several cylindrical flower buds that develop into large funnel-shaped blossoms. Unlike tiger lilies, the six-petaled flowers of daylilies are unspotted.

❦ *Fruit.* Several shiny black seeds develop inside pods at the tips of flower stalks.

HARVESTING DAYLILY

Daylily flower buds and flowers are available in midsummer throughout most of this plant's range. You can snap off flower buds with your fingers, or cut them off with a knife or scissors. Choose buds that are almost full-sized, just a couple of days before they would bloom. (Most flower stalks have a range of bud sizes, as well as a blooming flower, so you can easily judge the most desirable size to take.) The fully opened flowers and yesterday's withered blossoms are also edible.

Daylily tubers can be harvested year-round, even during the winter if the ground isn't frozen. Use a sturdy trowel or shovel to loosen the soil around the base of a cluster of daylily leaves. Grasp the leaves close to the ground and pull up, exposing the plant's cluster of tubers. Some are white, others are light brown, and most are about an inch long. Collect only the firm ones. After cutting several tubers from a cluster you can replant it, whether in the same or a new place. This will ensure future harvests of food, and more beautiful flowers.

Once you have located several clumps of daylilies, watch these places for the edible leaf sprouts in the spring. Cut some at ground level and discard the larger, outer leaves.

For a year-round supply of flower buds (or flowers), see the directions for drying in Having Wild Foods All Year.

DAY LILY   *Hemerocallis fulva*

tubers

You will find a dozen or more of these daylily tubers just a few inches underground, attached to the plant's long leaves.

CAUTION

The underground bulbs or roots of some plants are poisonous. This is true of iris, a smaller plant which grows near daylilies in some gardens or flower beds. One kind of iris is shown on page 65. Make sure the tubers you collect are attached to the easily identified daylily.

RECIPES

The young spring stalks, the tubers, and the flower buds can simply be steamed or boiled (see Cooking Tips, page 166). You can also add buds and flowers to salads, soups, stews, and mixed-vegetable dishes.

Young tubers, which are white and quite crisp, can be sliced raw into salads.

Daylily Buds Amandine

INGREDIENTS

2 cups daylily flower buds (fresh
   or well-soaked if dry)

2 tablespoons butter or margarine

1 cup sliced fresh mushrooms

1/2 cup slivered almonds

1 teaspoon soy sauce

EQUIPMENT

small saucepan

colander

measuring cup

measuring spoons

frying pan

Yield: 4 servings

1. Drop the flower buds into a pot of boiling salted water for about a minute, then drain.

2. Melt the butter in a frying pan. Add the mushrooms and flower buds. Sauté for a few minutes.

3. Add the almonds and the soy sauce, mixing well with the buds and mushrooms. Serve at once.

Daylily Fritters

INGREDIENTS

1 egg

1 cup milk

1 cup flour

1/2 teaspoon salt

1/8 teaspoon pepper

about 2 cups cooking oil

about 3 dozen fresh daylily flower
   buds

EQUIPMENT

medium mixing bowl

measuring cup

measuring spoons

medium saucepan

slotted spoon

paper towels

Yield: 4 to 6 servings

1. Mix the egg, milk, flour, salt, and pepper in a medium mixing bowl to make a thick batter.

2. Heat the oil in a saucepan over a moderate flame to about 375° F. To test, drop some batter into the oil. It should turn lightly brown in a few minutes.

3. Dip each flower bud in the batter, drop it into the hot oil, and fry to a golden brown. Do several at a time.

4. Remove with a slotted spoon. Drain the flowers on paper towels.

5. Serve as a vegetable dish, snack, dessert, or hors d'oeuvre. Try them sprinkled with salt or dipped in jam or sour cream.

Stir-Fried Daylily Buds

INGREDIENTS	EQUIPMENT
1 8-ounce can water chestnuts, drained	paring knife
	small mixing bowl
1 thin slice fresh ginger root	large frying pan or wok
1 teaspoon cornstarch	with cover
2 tablespoons peanut oil or corn oil	wooden spoon
2–3 cups daylily flower buds (fresh or well-soaked if dried)	
1 teaspoon salt	
1/4 teaspoon sugar	
1/4 cup water	

Yield: 4 servings

1. Before you start, have all ingredients handy. Slice the water chestnuts, chop the ginger root, and dissolve the cornstarch in 1 tablespoon of water.

2. Put a wok or heavy frying pan over high heat for 30 seconds. Pour in the oil and swirl it around.

3. Add the daylily buds and stir them constantly for a couple of minutes.

4. Add the water chestnuts, ginger root, salt, sugar, and water, and continue stirring.

5. Cover the pan and let the vegetables steam for 1 to 2 minutes.

6. Add the cornstarch-water mixture, and stir for about a half-minute. Serve at once.

Daylily Tubers and Dip

INGREDIENTS

about 50 daylily tubers

1/2 cup sour cream

1/2 cup mayonnaise

1 tablespoon red wine vinegar

salt and pepper to taste

EQUIPMENT

small brush (such as an old
   toothbrush)

vegetable steamer

medium saucepan

small mixing bowl

wooden toothpicks

Yield: 4 to 6 servings

1. To prepare the tubers, first cut off the rootlets. Then hold each tuber under a lightly running faucet and scrub off soil with a small brush.

2. Put the tubers in a steamer set in a saucepan with some water. Cover. Steam them over medium heat until they are tender (easily pierced with a fork).

3. Combine the sour cream, mayonnaise, vinegar, salt, and pepper in a small mixing bowl.

4. Stick a toothpick in each tuber and serve a bowl of tubers with the dip.

Lamb's-Quarters

❧ COMMON NAMES ❧

goosefoot, pigweed, wild spinach, fat hen, mealweed

❧ SCIENTIFIC NAME ❧

Chenopodium album *is the most common species.*

In Europe the use of lamb's-quarters as food has been traced back more than 1,700 years. Apparently it was cultivated long ago. Some people speculate that at one time early farmers may have pulled such weeds as wild wheat plants from their fields of lamb's-quarters! In any event, lamb's-quarters is still raised in some European gardens.

In North America, lamb's-quarters may be the most common wild edible plant; it has the potential for becoming much better known and much more widely used, because it has a mild taste and no poisonous parts. Related to spinach and beets, it is rich in calcium and vitamins A and C.

Lamb's-quarters often grows in gardens and cultivated fields, right alongside "tame" vegetables and
other wild foods, such as purslane (in foreground).

FINDING LAMB'S-QUARTERS

🌿 *Distribution.* Lamb's-quarters grows in all 50 states.
🌿 *Habitat.* Lamb's-quarters grows in gardens, cultivated fields, and
community leaf mulch piles, and along roadsides.

RECOGNIZING LAMB'S-QUARTERS

Appearance. A pale blue-green weed of open spaces.

Leaves. From one to four inches long, the leaves alternate on the stem; the oldest leaves, near the bottom of the plant, are bigger and broader than those near the top. Mature leaves look a little like the foot of a goose or duck, and also resemble the hind quarter of a lamb (something probably only a butcher would recognize). Leaf undersides are light-colored and have a gritty or powdery texture.

Flowers. Small green flowers grow in clusters near and at the top of the stem, and in the angles between the stem and leaf stalks.

Fruit. The seeds are dull black, tiny, and numerous—reportedly as many as 75,000 from a single plant.

Stems. Up to six feet tall, the stems are branched, ridged, sturdy, and striped with dark red near the ground.

HARVESTING LAMB'S-QUARTERS

Lamb's-quarters is available from mid-spring to the first frosts of autumn. Young plants up to a foot high can be picked and cooked whole. From older plants, pick the young tender leaves at the tips of the branches. You may want to wash the leaves before using them, but don't be repelled by their rather gritty feeling. What you feel is not dirt but a natural feature of the leaves. The seeds can be gathered in the fall by putting a pail or a wide-mouthed plastic container beneath a plant and rubbing the stem over the container so that the seeds fall in. Though tiny, the seeds are so abundant that you can collect several cupfuls in a short time.

RECIPES

Young lamb's-quarter leaves are good raw in salads, while older leaves can be added to soups and stews. Old or young, the

LAMB'S QUARTERS

Chenopodium album

seeds

leaves can be steamed or boiled for a few minutes (see Cooking Tips, page 166), then served with butter and salt, or with a sprinkling of vinegar. When ground, the seeds make a nutritious flour; they can also be put in a little water and boiled until soft, then eaten as a breakfast cereal.

Sweet and Sour Lamb's-Quarters

INGREDIENTS	EQUIPMENT
4 slices bacon	large frying pan
8 cups lamb's-quarter leaves, rinsed and finely chopped	paper towels
	sharp knife
1 medium onion, finely chopped	measuring cup
2 cups boiling water	measuring spoons
1 tart apple, peeled, cored, and diced	
2 tablespoons flour	
4 tablespoons brown sugar	
2 tablespoons vinegar	

Yield: 6 to 8 servings
1. Fry the bacon until crisp, and then drain on paper towels.
2. Put the leaves in the bacon fat and sauté for 8 to 10 minutes.
3. Add the onion and cook until it is lightly browned.
4. Pour the boiling water and the apple into the lamb's-quarter mixture.
5. Simmer until the apple pieces are tender.
6. Sprinkle with the flour, brown sugar, and vinegar. Simmer for 5 to 10 minutes more.
7. Serve hot, with the bacon crumbled on top.

Lamb's-Quarter Cheese Snacks

INGREDIENTS	EQUIPMENT
8 cups lamb's-quarter leaves	vegetable steamer
2 eggs, lightly beaten	colander
1 1/2 cups bread crumbs	sharp knife
1/2 cup grated cheddar cheese	medium mixing bowl
2 tablespoons finely chopped onion	small mixing bowl
1 tablespoon lemon juice	eggbeater or electric mixer
1 teaspoon salt	grater
about 2 cups cooking oil	measuring cup
salt	measuring spoons
	large saucepan
	slotted spoon
	paper towels

Yield: 6 to 8 servings

1. Steam the lamb's-quarters until tender. Drain well in a colander.
2. Chop the leaves finely and put them in a mixing bowl.
3. Add the eggs to the lamb's-quarters.
4. Mix in the bread crumbs, cheese, onion, lemon juice, and salt.
5. In a large saucepan heat the cooking oil to about 375° F.
6. Make bite-sized balls of the mixture and drop them into the hot oil. If they do not hold together in the oil, add some more bread crumbs to the mixture. Fry a few at a time until crisp and lightly browned.
7. Remove with a slotted spoon and drain on paper towels. Sprinkle with salt and serve immediately.

Lamb's-Quarter Quiche

INGREDIENTS

1 homemade or store-bought 9-inch
   pie crust

2 tablespoons butter or margarine

4 cups lamb's-quarter leaves, rinsed
   and chopped

1/4 cup chopped onion

1 tablespoon flour

1/2 teaspoon salt

3 eggs

1 3/4 cups milk

2 cups grated Swiss cheese
   (8 ounces)

EQUIPMENT

9-inch pie plate

sharp knife

medium saucepan

measuring cup

measuring spoons

grater

large mixing bowl

eggbeater or electric mixer

Yield: 6 servings

1. Partially bake the pie crust in a 450° F oven for about 5 minutes, until it is lightly browned. Take it out of the oven and reduce the heat to 325° F.

2. Melt the butter in a saucepan, add the lamb's-quarters and onion, and cook for about 5 minutes, until the leaves are limp and the onion is tender.

3. Mix in the flour and salt.

4. In a large bowl, beat together the eggs and milk. Add the cooked onion and lamb's-quarters.

5. Sprinkle the grated cheese on the bottom of the pie crust, then pour in the egg-vegetable mixture.

6. Bake in a preheated oven for 40–45 minutes. The filling should be firm and custardlike by then. To test, stick a knife into the center of

the quiche; if it comes out clean, the quiche is done. Let it cool for 10 minutes before serving.

Lamb's-Quarter Seed Bread

INGREDIENTS

1/2 cup ground lamb's-quarter seed

1/2 cup cornmeal

3/4 cup whole-wheat flour

2 teaspoons baking powder

1/4 teaspoon salt

1/2 cup plus 1 tablespoon water

1 tablespoon honey

2 tablespoons cooking oil

1 egg yolk

EQUIPMENT

blender or other grinding device

measuring cup

measuring spoons

medium mixing bowl

baking sheet

small mixing bowl

pastry brush

Yield: one small loaf

1. Make sure the seeds are dry. (If necessary, dry them for a half-hour in a 200° F oven.) Then grind them as finely as possible in a blender or coffee grinder, or with a mortar and pestle.
2. Preheat the oven to 350° F.
3. In a medium mixing bowl, combine the ground seeds, cornmeal, flour, baking powder, and salt.
4. Add 1/2 cup of water, the honey, and the oil. Mix thoroughly.
5. Form the dough into a ball-shaped loaf, and put it on a greased baking sheet.
6. Mix the egg yolk and the remaining 1 tablespoon of water. Brush this mixture onto the surface of the loaf.
7. Bake in the preheated oven for 25 to 35 minutes. Serve hot, with butter.

Purslane

❧ COMMON NAMES ❧
pursley, pusley, wild portulaca

❧ SCIENTIFIC NAME ❧
Portulaca oleracea

Until 1975, purslane was considered a foreign plant in North America. Its use had been traced back more than 2,000 years in Persia and India. However, purslane seeds and pollen have been found buried in Canadian sediments that were laid down well before Columbus "discovered" America. It seems that purslane is a native plant after all.

Each year many tons of purslane are weeded from gardens. Some people feel this is a terrible waste; they like the slightly acid taste of the purslane "weed" as well or better than some of the vegetables that remain in gardens. A few foragers, myself included, have transplanted purslane to their home gardens in order to have a supply handy.

Look for purslane (right) in gardens and in farmer's field.

FINDING PURSLANE

❧ *Distribution.* Purslane grows in all 50 states.

❧ *Habitat.* Purslane grows in gardens, cultivated fields, and other areas of fertile, dry soil.

RECOGNIZING PURSLANE

❧ *Appearance.* A creeping, low-growing plant, purslane sometimes almost covers the soil with a mat of stems and small leaves.

❧ *Leaves.* No more than an inch long, purslane leaves are simple and somewhat paddle-shaped, with rounded tips. They are fleshy and succulent (made of special water-storing tissues).

❧ *Flowers.* Tiny yellow flowers with five petals develop at the places where stems fork. The flowers bloom only in bright morning sunlight.

❧ *Stems.* Near their roots, purslane stems are about 1/4 inch in diameter. Near their growing tips the smooth reddish stems are smaller.

PURSLANE
Portulaca oleracea

HARVESTING PURSLANE

Purslane is available from late spring until the first frosts of autumn. The entire plant is edible. If you just pluck off the tips of stems, new growth will replace them and provide you with further crops. Since purslane creeps over bare soil, it should be thoroughly rinsed before using.

RECIPES

Purslane can be used raw in salads. One combination you should try: purslane, mint, and watercress salad. Purslane can also be cooked in stews or soups, or steamed and served with butter, salt, and pepper. Purslane stems and tips can also be pickled (see Having Wild Foods All Year). Unlike spinach, lamb's-quarters, and other greens, purslane does not shrink much in size when cooked.

Purslane Dip

INGREDIENTS

1 cup purslane

1 teaspoon minced onion

1 pint sour cream

1 small container red caviar

salt and pepper to taste

Tabasco sauce (optional)

EQUIPMENT

sharp knife

mixing bowl

Yield: 6 to 8 servings
1. Rinse the purslane and chop it finely.
2. Mix with the onions, sour cream, and caviar.
3. Taste the dip, and add salt, pepper, and 2 drops of Tabasco sauce if you like.
4. Refrigerate for an hour before serving.

Purslane Casserole

INGREDIENTS	EQUIPMENT
6 cups purslane leaves and young stems	measuring cup
	measuring spoons
1/2 teaspoon salt	medium saucepan
3 cups water	colander
2 tablespoons butter	sharp knife
1/2 cup finely chopped onion	large saucepan
1/2 pound thinly sliced mushrooms	1 1/2-quart baking dish
1/4 teaspoon pepper	small mixing bowl
1/4 teaspoon nutmeg	
1/2 cup heavy cream	
2 eggs	
2 egg yolks	

Yield: 4 to 6 servings

1. Preheat the oven to 400° F.
2. In a saucepan heat about 3 cups of water to boiling. Add the salt and purslane. Reduce heat, cover, and cook for about 5 minutes.
3. Drain the purslane in a colander and let it cool. Chop it coarsely.
4. Melt the butter in a large saucepan. Add the onion and cook for 3 minutes until wilted.
5. Add the mushrooms and pepper and continue cooking until the mushrooms begin to shrink.
6. Add the purslane and cook about 3 minutes. Add the nutmeg and mix it in thoroughly.
7. Pour the mixture into a baking dish.
8. In a small mixing bowl combine the cream, eggs, and egg yolks. Pour this mixture over the vegetables.

9. Bake in the preheated oven for about 20 minutes, then serve immediately.

Purslane Soup

INGREDIENTS

1 tablespoon butter

2 cups chopped purslane

1/2 cup finely chopped onion

1/2 cup white wine

4 cups light cream

salt, pepper, and paprika to taste

EQUIPMENT

sharp knife

medium saucepan

measuring cup

measuring spoons

Yield: 4 servings

1. Melt the butter in a saucepan, add the purslane and onion, and sauté for a few minutes.
2. Add the wine and boil. Then add cream and seasonings to taste.
3. Heat through but *do not boil*. Serve the soup hot.

Purslane Quiche

Follow the recipe for lamb's-quarter quiche (page 138), substituting 2 cups of purslane leaves and stems for the lamb's-quarter leaves.

Yield: 6 servings

Wild Blueberry

❦ COMMON NAMES ❦

black highbush blueberry, common highbush blueberry, bilberry, whortleberry, deerberry, slender blueberry, early lowbush blueberry, late lowbush blueberry

❦ SCIENTIFIC NAMES ❦

There are more than thirty North American species, all in the genus Vaccinium.

Juicy and sweet, blueberries are among our finest wild fruits. The wild bushes sometimes cover many acres of land. Blueberries are also raised commercially, but these big berries tend to be pulpy and lacking in flavor, compared with their smaller wild ancestors. The wild berries also work better in recipes for pies, muffins, and other baked goods because their skins do not burst as easily as "tame" blueberries.

North American Indians used blueberries a lot, and dried them for winter and spring food. You can do the same (see Having Wild Foods All Year for drying instructions). Dried blueberries are a good substitute for raisins, as a snack or in recipes that call for raisins.

Ripe blueberries are often coated with a harmless white "bloom."

FINDING WILD BLUEBERRY

❧ *Distribution.* Blueberry species grow in the original 48 states and in Alaska.

❧ *Habitat.* Some species grow in wet, boggy places and along the shores of lakes; others thrive in dry, sandy soils.

RECOGNIZING WILD BLUEBERRY

❧ *Appearance.* Woody shrubs. As some of their common names suggest, blueberry species vary a lot in size. Some of the highbush kinds grow to be fifteen feet tall, while lowbush varieties reach only about twenty inches.

❧ *Leaves.* All blueberry species have short-stalked simple leaves from one to three inches long. Some species have toothed edges, while others are smooth.

❧ *Flowers.* The white flowers are about 1/4 inch long and bell-shaped.

❧ *Fruit.* About 1/4 to 1/2 inch in diameter, blueberries seem dusted with white. This harmless "bloom," as it is called, comes off wherever you touch a berry. Each blueberry contains many seeds, so tiny and soft that you hardly notice them. If you *do* notice them, you are probably chewing a huckleberry (of the genus *Gaylussacia*). Huckleberries contain ten hard seedlike nutlets. Huckleberry bushes resemble blueberry bushes, and fortunately their fruit is also safe and delicious.

❧ *Stems.* Mature stems are brown and woody; twigs are slender, green or reddish, and speckled with many little raised bumps.

HARVESTING WILD BLUEBERRY

Blueberries ripen in the summer, the time varying with the species and the climate. Blueberry crops also vary with the climate. One year the berries may be small and scarce, while the next year they may be big and so plentiful that you can strip them off a bush ten at a time. Blueberry bushes are not thorny, but you should still wear long pants while picking and take along some insect repellent.

Some foraging books recommend putting a large plastic or cloth sheet under a heavily laden blueberry bush, then simply shaking the berries off. You might want to use this method, although the one time I did try it many ripe berries stayed on the bush, and those that did fall off were mixed with leaves, twigs, and unripe berries.

One of the best containers to use for berry picking is an empty one-gallon plastic milk jug, the kind with a handle. Using scissors, cut away a section of the jug opposite the handle. One advantage of this container: you can run your belt through the jug's handle so that the jug hangs at your waist, leaving both hands free.

BLUEBERRY *Vaccinium*

RECIPES

Like strawberries and raspberries, wild blueberries can be eaten raw in many ways: straight from the bush, sprinkled on cereal or ice cream, mixed with yogurt, or in a bowl with cream and sugar.

Blueberry Soup

INGREDIENTS	EQUIPMENT
2 1/2 cups wild blueberries	medium saucepan
1/4 cup sugar	measuring cup
1 tablespoon lemon juice	measuring spoons
1 tablespoon flour	small mixing bowl
1 tablespoon cold water	wooden spoon
1/2 cup heavy cream	blender
	fine-mesh sieve

Yield: 4 servings

1. In a medium saucepan, mix together the berries, sugar, and lemon juice, and bring to a boil.
2. In a small bowl mix the flour and water into a smooth paste. Add to the blueberries.
3. Reduce the heat and simmer for 5 minutes. Let cool.
4. Pour into the blender, purée the soup, then pour through the sieve.
5. Chill in the refrigerator. Add the heavy cream just before serving. Serve cold.

Wild-Blueberry Uncooked Jam

Follow the recipe for wild-strawberry jam on page 75. For 4 cups of blueberries, use 4 cups of sugar or less.

Blueberry Ices

Follow the recipe on page 123 substituting blueberries for raspberries.

Blueberry Crisp Pudding

INGREDIENTS	EQUIPMENT
4 tablespoons butter or margarine	1 1/2-quart baking dish
4 cups wild blueberries	measuring cup
1/2 cup white sugar	measuring spoons
1 tablespoon lemon juice	medium mixing bowl
1/3 cup firmly packed brown sugar	wire whisk
1/2 teaspoon cinnamon	eggbeater or electric mixer
1/3 cup flour	(optional)
3/4 cup granola cereal	
1/2 cup heavy cream, whipped	
(optional)	
ice cream (optional)	

Yield: 6 to 8 servings

1. Let the butter soften in a mixing bowl at room temperature.
2. Preheat the oven to 375° F.
3. Spread the blueberries evenly in the baking dish. Sprinkle on the white sugar and lemon juice.
4. With a whisk cream the butter. Then add the brown sugar and mix well.
5. Mix in the cinnamon, flour, and granola.
6. Spread this mixture over the berries.
7. Bake in the preheated oven for about 40 minutes. Serve with whipped cream or ice cream if you like.

Sumac

❧ COMMON NAMES ❧

staghorn sumac, smooth sumac, dwarf sumac, squaw bush, lemonade tree, scarlet sumac

❧ SCIENTIFIC NAMES ❧

Rhus typhina *(staghorn)*, Rhus glabra *(smooth)*, Rhus copallina *(dwarf)*, Rhus trilobata *(squaw bush)* are some common species.

The name sumac may come from the German word *schuhmacher* (shoemaker) because sumac was once used by shoemakers to tan leather. Indians gathered the seed clusters, dried them, and made a lemonadelike drink from them in the wintertime. Settlers from Europe also learned to make "Indian lemonade." The tart taste comes from malic acid on the red hairs of the fruit clusters. Of all the sumacs, staghorn has the greatest amount of acid because it has the longest hairs (about two millimeters long). Malic acid is also present in unripe apples.

The bright red seed mass of smooth sumac, shown
here, is not as "furry" looking as that of staghorn sumac.

FINDING SUMAC

🌿 *Distribution.* Sumac species occur in nearly all of the United
States, including Hawaii.

🌿 *Habitat.* Sumac grows in the dry soil in fields and thickets and
along roads and the edges of forests.

RECOGNIZING SUMAC

Appearance. Shrubs or small trees, seldom more than 20 feet tall, usually growing in clumps.

Leaves. The pinnately compound leaves are made up of two-to-five-inch lance-shaped leaflets. The number of leaflets vary; staghorn sumac has from 11 to 31 leaflets making up each leaf.

Flowers. Small green flowers grow in a tight cluster, often several inches long.

Fruit. Female flower clusters develop into erect, cone-shaped masses of dry red fruits.

Stems. The bark of mature stems is dark gray. Staghorn sumac has very hairy twigs, the hair resembling the velvet fuzz on developing deer antlers—hence the name staghorn. Smooth sumac is much like staghorn sumac but its twigs are hairless. Sumac twigs have a soft core of pith that can be poked out in order to make spiles for collecting maple sap.

CAUTION

The sumac genus, *Rhus*, includes three rather nasty relatives—poison ivy, poison oak, and poison sumac. All of them contain an oil that is a serious skin irritant for many people. Of the three, only poison sumac *(Rhus vernix)* bears much of a resemblance to the other sumacs. It grows in swamps, however, not in dry open places. It has hairless buds and twigs, and its leaflets are not toothed on their edges. Its drooping clusters of berries are yellowish-white. There is little danger that you will encounter this plant if you collect only clusters of red sumac berries.

HARVESTING SUMAC

The malic acid on sumac fruit dissolves easily in water. This results in some good news and some bad news. First, the good news:

STAGHORN SUMAC *Rhus typhina*

~ *fruit clusters* ~

STAGHORN   SMOOTH   ☠ POISON SUMAC

the solubility of malic acid in water makes it easy for you to make Indian lemonade. Now the bad: rain gradually washes the acid away, and the fruit clusters are less useful for making beverages after a couple of rainstorms. This means that you should collect sumac fruit clusters soon after they mature, in mid to late summer—a time when a cool lemony drink is most welcome anyway. Collecting them soon after they mature also reduces the chance that they might be infested with insects.

But first, cut off just a few of the bright red masses. Carry the clusters home in a plastic bag or paper sack. If you like the taste of Indian lemonade, you can then gather many more fruit clusters and dry them (see Having Wild Foods All Year) for use in the wintertime. (Because of the water solubility of malic acid, however, do not wash the sumac before drying.)

RECIPES

Sumacade or Indian Lemonade

INGREDIENTS	EQUIPMENT
about 10 cups sumac berries	large pot or saucepan
5 quarts cold water	sharp knife
sugar or honey to taste	large spoon or potato masher
	old T-shirt or cheesecloth
	colander

Yield: about 20 servings

1. *Do not wash* the berry clusters. Cut the berries from their stems. Put them in a large pot with the cold water.*

> *Do not put entire fruit clusters into hot water because it will release a bitter taste from the sumac stems. Use hot water only if you cut all the stems from the berries.

2. Bruise and mash the berries for several minutes, until the water turns pink. Let them soak for a half-hour or more.
3. To remove the berries and fine hairs, strain the mixture through an old, clean T-shirt or several layers of cheesecloth set in a colander.
4. Add sugar to taste, chill, and serve.

Sumacade can also be served as a hot tea. In the fall or winter, dried sumac berries can be made into a fine warming drink:

Mulled Sumacade

INGREDIENTS

8 cups sumacade

8 whole cloves

2 sticks cinnamon

1 teaspoon ground allspice

1/2 cup firmly packed brown sugar

1 lemon, sliced

1 orange, sliced

freshly grated nutmeg

EQUIPMENT

large saucepan

sharp knife

grater

Yield: 8 to 10 servings
1. After making the sumacade from dried berries, put it in a large saucepan.
2. Add the cloves, cinnamon, allspice, brown sugar, and lemon and orange slices.
3. Heat the mixture over low heat for 30 minutes. Do not boil.
4. Serve it hot, topped with nutmeg.

Wild Grape

❦ COMMON NAMES ❦

fox grape, summer grape, frost grape, dune grape, canyon grape, mustang grape, bush grape

❦ SCIENTIFIC NAMES ❦

Vitis labrusca *(fox),* Vitis arizonica *(canyon),* Vitis vulpina *(frost),* and Vitis rotundifolia *(muscadine) are some common North American species.*

The two dozen species of wild grapes in North America are related to the wine grape *(Vitis vinifera)* of Europe, from which most grape wine is made. In North America the fox grape is the wild ancestor of such cultivated varieties as Concord, Catawba, and Chautauqua.

At one time it was believed that Viking explorers called North America "Vinland" because they found wild grapes where they settled briefly, in what is now northern Newfoundland. However, no wild grapes grow there. Botanists now believe that Leif Ericson found the grapelike fruits of the mountain cranberry *(Vaccinium vitisidaea).*

Late summer and early autumn is harvest time for wild grapes.

FINDING WILD GRAPE

🌿 *Distribution.* Wild grape species occur in the original 48 states and in Alaska.

🌿 *Habitat.* Wild grape grows in the fertile soil of thickets, roadsides, and the edges of forests.

RECOGNIZING WILD GRAPE

🌿 *Appearance.* Wild-grape vines can climb a hundred feet into the canopy of a forest, and also blanket an area of ground and shrubs.

🌿 *Leaves.* The leaves have toothed edges, are usually heart-shaped, and grow up to eight inches across. They grow opposite one another. The undersides of some species' leaves have dense growths of fine hairs, while others are hairless.

🌿 *Flowers.* Clusters of fragrant green flowers develop in early summer.

🌿 *Fruit.* Ripe grapes may be red, purple, black, or green. They are fleshy and contain several hard, small seeds. The flavor varies from species to species, some being quite sweet, others bitter.

🌿 *Stems.* Wild-grape vines climb by means of springlike growths called tendrils. Young vines are smooth and light green; older ones have gray-brown bark that comes off in strips.

CAUTION

Wild grapes resemble moonseed *(Menispermum canadense)*, a rare poisonous plant of the northeastern United States. Moonseed fruits grow in grapelike clusters and ripen about the same time as grapes. The leaves are quite similar to grape leaves. But there are two major differences. Unlike grapes, the fruit of moonseed contains just one crescent-shaped seed. Notice also how the vine climbs. Moonseed vines twine around and around objects, while grape vines cling by tendrils.

Other vines with inedible fruits resemble wild grapes in some ways. Virginia creeper *(Parthenocissus quinquefolia)* has clusters of grapelike fruits but has five leaflets arranged like a fan (palmately compound). American ampelopsis *(Ampelopsis cordata)* has grapelike leaves but its blueish fruits are pea-sized, hard, and dry.

HARVESTING WILD GRAPE

Pick young grape leaves in the late spring and early summer when they are full-sized but still light green. Later in the season they become rather tough and bitter.

Grapes ripen in late summer and early autumn. Cut one open to be sure it has several seeds and not just the single big seed of moonseed (see above). Taste the grapes you find, but don't be repelled by a strong, tart flavor. Tart kinds can be made into delicious pies, jelly, and juice. Cut the clusters free with a knife or scissors.

WILD GRAPE *Vitis*

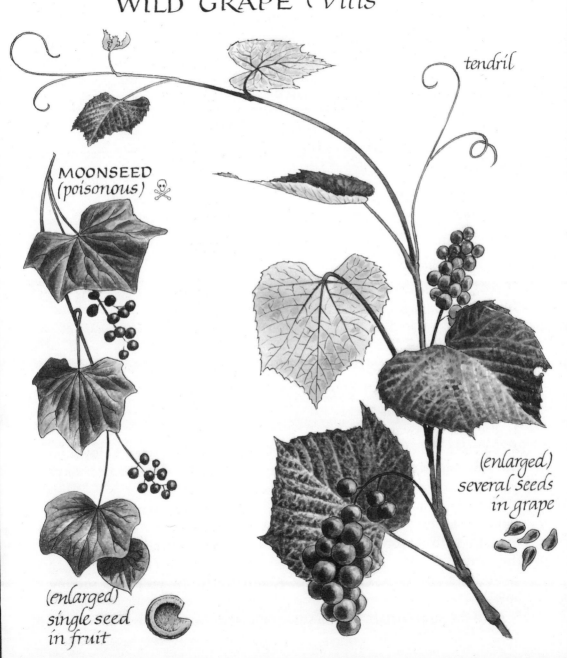

tendril

MOONSEED
(poisonous) ☠

(enlarged)
several seeds
in grape

(enlarged)
single seed
in fruit

RECIPES

Tender grape leaves can be steamed and served with butter and salt. Their delicate acid flavor has been part of Middle Eastern cuisine for many centuries. One recipe for stuffed grape leaves is included here; in cookbooks you will find recipes for many other stuffings.

Wild Grape Pie

INGREDIENTS	EQUIPMENT
4 cups wild grapes, stemmed and washed	*medium saucepan*
	fine-mesh sieve or strainer
1 cup sugar	*wooden spoon*
4 tablespoons flour	*sharp knife*
1 teaspoon lemon juice	*measuring cup*
1/4 teaspoon salt	*measuring spoons*
1 tablespoon butter	*9-inch pie plate*
1 homemade or store-bought double-crust pastry for a 9-inch pie	

Yield: one 9-inch pie

1. Preheat the oven to 400° F.
2. Squeeze the pulp from the skins of the grapes by pressing down on the side opposite the hole where the stems had been attached. Save the skins.
3. Put the pulp in a saucepan and heat to a rolling boil. Let it cool somewhat, then put the pulp into a fine-mesh sieve and mash it through with a wooden spoon, forcing the pulp through but leaving the seeds.
4. Finely chop the reserved skins. Add them to the pulp in a mixing bowl.
5. Add the sugar, flour, lemon juice, and salt. Mix well.

6. Pour this mixture into the uncooked pie crust. Dot the top of the pie filling with butter.

7. Cover with the top crust, and squeeze the edges of the top and bottom crusts together. Press with the tines of a fork all around the pie's edge, making a tight seal.

8. Make several knife slits in the top crust to allow steam to escape.

9. Place the pie in the middle rack of the oven and bake in the preheated oven for 35 to 45 minutes, until the top crust is lightly browned and juice bubbles from the slits. Serve while still warm.

Wild Grape Jelly

INGREDIENTS	EQUIPMENT
about 3 pounds of wild grapes	10 jelly jars, sterilized
1/2 cup water	shallow pan
1/4 cup lemon juice	small saucepan
4 cups sugar*	sharp knife
1/2 bottle (3 ounces) fruit pectin	2 large stainless-steel or enamel
paraffin	saucepans
	jelly bag
	medium mixing bowl
	measuring cup
	measuring spoons

*Since the sweetness of wild grapes varies considerably, the amount of sugar used can also vary. Taste some of the grapes you are going to use for jelly, to determine their sweetness, and experiment with the amount of sweetening.

Yield: about 10 small jars of jelly

1. The procedure for making wild-grape jelly is mostly the same described for wild-mint jelly (pages 114–115). Follow the directions there

for sterilizing jars and preparing the paraffin.

2. Remove the grapes from their stems and wash them. They needn't all be ripe, but discard rotten or moldy ones. Crush the grapes in a large saucepan. Add 1/2 cup water and bring to a boil.

3. Reduce the heat and simmer the grapes for 10 minutes.

4. Put the cooled grapes and their juice in a jelly bag set over a medium mixing bowl. Let the juice drip through overnight. In the morning carefully pour or dip the juice from the bowl, being careful not to include any of the sediments or crystals that are in the bowl.

5. Measure 3 1/2 cups of the grape juice and put it in a large stainless-steel or enamel saucepan. Add the lemon juice and sugar. Mix well.

6. Put over high heat and bring to a boil, stirring constantly. Stir in the pectin. Bring to a full rolling boil and boil for 1 minute, stirring constantly.

7. Remove from heat, skim off foam with a metal spoon, and pour quickly into sterilized jars. Cover at once with a 1/8-inch layer of melted paraffin.

Stuffed Wild-Grape Leaves

INGREDIENTS	EQUIPMENT
60 to 70 young grape leaves (about 4–5 inches across)	sharp knife
	2 large saucepans
5–5 1/2 cups water	colander
pinch of salt	measuring cup
1 pound ground lamb	measuring spoons
2 cups converted rice, cooked but firm	medium bowl
2 tablespoons finely chopped parsley	

INGREDIENTS

2 tablespoons finely chopped dill

1/2 teaspoon chopped fresh rosemary

  or crushed dried rosemary

1 teaspoon salt

1/4 teaspoon pepper

Yield: 6 to 8 servings

1. Trim the stems from the leaves. In a saucepan bring 4 cups of lightly salted water to a boil and add the leaves. Boil for 5 minutes. Drain the leaves in a colander.

2. In a medium bowl mix all of the other ingredients for the stuffing.

3. Place a grape leaf on a flat surface with the stem end facing you and its smooth upper side down. Put 1 tablespoon of the stuffing an inch from the base of the leaf. Roll the bottom third of the leaf around the stuffing, then fold in the right and left sides of the leaf. Finish by rolling the stuffing up in the rest of the leaf, rolling away from you. Don't roll too tightly because the rice may expand a bit. Roll leaves this way until all of the stuffing is used up.

4. Place the stuffed leaves in a large saucepan with their seam edges down, one atop the other in several layers. Add the remaining 1 to 1 1/2 cups of water. Cover the pan.

5. Cook over medium heat for about 45 minutes. (Stuffed grape leaves can also be baked in a 350°F oven for an hour.) Serve hot or chilled.

Cooking Tips

ABOUT SUGAR AND HONEY

Recipes in this book usually call for use of granulated white sugar rather than honey. Some people may choose to use honey because they believe it is better for their health. Most nutritionists believe that honey is somewhat superior nutritionally to granulated white sugar, but that the less sweetening of any kind—including honey—you use, the better off you'll be.

Unfortunately there is no simple rule for honey-sugar substitution, since honey itself varies (depending on the kind of flowers from which it was made, and other factors). Often you can substitute about 3/4 to 7/8 cup of honey for 1 cup of granulated white sugar. If you decide to use honey, you may have to experiment with the kinds that are available in your area, and/or seek the advice of someone who has experience in honey-sugar substitution.

ABOUT BOILING AND STEAMING

Many of the edible plants in this book can be prepared as cooked vegetables, either boiled or steamed. Steaming is preferable, because when plant parts are steamed, most of the available vitamins and minerals are retained within the plant parts you are cooking. If you boil vegetables, use as little water as possible, serve them in the liquid that remains, and make sure the liquid is consumed, since this "pot liquor," as it is called, contains nutrients that were boiled out of the vegetables.

An inexpensive collapsible vegetable steamer makes steaming easy. Place it in a saucepan containing about 1/2 inch of water, and put the vegetables in the steamer. Bring the water to a boil, put some butter or margarine on top of the vegetables, cover the pan, reduce the heat, and steam the vegetables until tender. When they are easily pierced with a fork, turn off the heat and use a potholder to remove the steamer from the pan. Put the vegetables in a serving dish and pour the buttery liquid from the pan over them. Add more butter, salt, pepper, and other seasonings if you like.

If you don't have a steamer, lay the vegetables in a big frying pan containing a small amount of water to which you have added a few dashes of salt and some butter. Bring the water to a boil, cover the pan, and let the vegetables simmer until tender (test occasionally with a fork). Don't let all of the water boil away. Then drain the vegetables by pouring them into a colander set in the sink. Put them in a serving dish, and add additional butter and whatever seasonings you like.

ABOUT SEASONINGS

One of the delights of wild foods is their just-picked flavor. To complement and enhance this taste, whenever possible use fresh seasonings and other ingredients—for example, freshly ground pepper and freshly squeezed lemon juice.

Having Wild Foods All Year

Foraging for wild foods need not stop at the end of summer. Several kinds of edible plants are available until, or even after, the first frost. If the climate is mild or moderate where you live, you can probably find some wild edible plants in the midst of winter. In colder climates, such wild foods as walnuts and hickory nuts can be gathered after freezing temperatures have killed the tender leaves of sorrel and wild mint. Like some other wild foods, nuts are most abundant and tasty during a rather brief part of the year. Collect them soon after they fall from trees, before they begin to decay or are carried off by other foragers — squirrels.

By the time you read these words, I hope you have already found some wild foods whose taste you like. If so, you will probably enjoy "putting some by," and having the pleasures of wild summer tastes in the deep of winter. On the following pages you will find some tips about how to have wild foods in wintertime.

A WILD WINTER GARDEN

Some wild edible plants can be kept alive and well and producing meals in winter if you protect them from the cold. This works best with such plants as dandelion, plantain, sheep sorrel, and poke. You may want to experiment with others.

You can make your wild winter garden by using an existing patch of edible plants or by transplanting the species you want to a convenient place near your home. Your goal is to create a mild microclimate at ground level so that the plants keep producing tender new leaves and sprouts. Several inches of straw or dead leaves placed over the plants will insulate them from the cold. Insulation is also provided by snow if it falls on top of the straw. The depth of straw or leaves needed will vary with the climate of different regions, and with the severity of the winter.

You can also set up a wild garden indoors in winter. This has been done successfully with several plants, including dandelion and poke, which normally produce sprouts or leaves in early-to-mid spring. Dig up roots of the plants you want and place them in a box, tub, or other container of soil. Remember, poke root is poisonous to eat; it is young sprouts from the root you want. If a poke root is too big to fit into a container of soil, cut off some of its lower part. Barely cover the top of the roots with soil. Leave the containers outdoors until they have been exposed to a few weeks of freezing temperatures. Then set up your garden in a warm, dark place such as the cellar or a closet. Keep the soil well watered, and wait for wild vegetables to grow.

The roots will not produce new growth indefinitely, since they are using up stored food. If you anticipate wanting a steady supply of wild sprouts and leaves throughout the winter, you will need to prepare several containers of soil and roots. Then you can bring new little gardens indoors after others stop producing crops.

MAKING FRUIT LEATHER

An unusual way to preserve wild fruits is to change them into thin, flat sheets called fruit leather. The sheets are a delicious and handy snack on hikes and picnics. You can make fruit leather from strawberries, raspberries, blackberries, blueberries, wild grapes, and also from finely chopped stalks of Japanese knotweed (the tender stalks which are used for pies).

Put the fruit in a large saucepan or pot with a small amount of orange or pineapple juice (use about 1 cup of juice to a gallon of fruit). You will need to crush blueberries with a wooden spoon or a potato masher in order to break the skins of the berries. In the case of wild grapes, squeeze the pulp from their skins, force the pulp through a sieve to remove the seeds, then combine the pulp with the finely chopped grape skins.

Cook the fruit over low heat, stirring occasionally, until it thickens. Taste the fruit and sweeten with honey or sugar if you want. Then spread it as thinly as possible on lightly oiled cookie sheets. Dry in the oven at about 120° F, with the oven door open slightly to allow moisture to escape.

When the fruit leather is dry enough so that you can easily lift an edge from the cookie sheet, put it on a cake rack at room temperature so it dries more on both sides. When it no longer feels sticky, dust both sides lightly with cornstarch. Store in a cool, dry place with sheets of wax paper or clear plastic wrap between layers. Fruit leather can be stored at room temperature for about a month or in the refrigerator for about four months.

DRYING

Although freezing is the preferred method of preserving most wild fruits, such hard-skinned fruits as blueberries, huckleberries, and elderberries are fine when dried. Use fully ripe, thoroughly washed berries that are free of blemishes and bruises. Place them in a sieve, dip them into boiling water for 15 to 30 seconds, then into cold water. After the berries drain thoroughly, spread them out on a cookie sheet on which you have made a "tray" of aluminum foil with upturned edges so the berries don't roll off. Dry them in a 120° F oven. After an hour, increase the heat to 140° F. Drying should take 4 hours or less. Thoroughly dry berries will rattle when you shake the cookie sheet.

Allow the berries to cool, then store them in small, tightly sealed plastic bags. Put the bags in large containers with tight lids and keep in a cool, dry, dark place. To use the berries, put them in a saucepan, add just enough boiling water to cover them, cover the pan, and let them soak for several hours, until all of the berries are tender. When you use the berries, don't discard the liquid, since it is full of vitamins and minerals.

Among the plants described in this book, the leaves of strawberry, raspberry, blackberry, and wild mint can be dried for tea-making. For best results, dry the leaves in the air, in the dark, and at temperatures no higher than 100° F. One method: put bunches of leaves in a large brown paper bag, tie the top loosely, and hang the bag in a warm, dry room. If you dry leaves in the oven, keep the temperature at 120° F or less.

Test for dryness by crumbling a leaf; thoroughly dry leaves are easy to crumble. Package them in air-tight containers and store in a dry, dark place.

Such wild greens as lambs'-quarters, dandelion, plantain, purslane, and sheep sorrel can also be dried. Steam the leaves for about 5 minutes, let them drain, then spread them in a very thin layer on cookie sheets. Dry in the oven at about 140° F, with the door slightly ajar. When the leaves crumble easily, let them cool, then store them as you would dried berries. To prepare for use, cover the dried greens with boiling water and simmer until tender.

FREEZING

Many of the wild foods in this book can be preserved by freezing. Such vegetables as dandelion leaves, poke sprouts, and milkweed flowers and seed pods can be frozen. Freezing is also the best way to preserve such soft fruits as strawberries and raspberries.

Leaves and other vegetable parts should be steamed or plunged into boiling water for a few minutes, then cooled in cold water, thoroughly drained, and stored in sturdy plastic bags or other containers and sealed tightly. In jars and plastic boxes leave at least a half-inch of space to allow for expansion of the food as it freezes. Label the packages, indicating the kind of food and the date of freezing. Use the oldest frozen vegetables first. Frozen greens and vegetables need not be thawed before cooking.

Fruits can be frozen either of two ways: dry, or in a sweet syrup. If you choose to freeze berries dry, make sure that they are dry on their outer surfaces. Some foragers say that they get best results when they first spread berries in a single layer on a tray in the freezer, then pack the frozen fruit in containers. This way the berries do not stick together, an advantage when you want to use only part of the berries in a container.

A sweet syrup for berries can be made by briefly boiling together 2 parts of water to 1 part sugar, or 3 parts of water to 1 part of a mild-flavored honey. Let the syrup cool before adding it to the berries. Leave about an inch of space at the top of wide-top containers and more for narrow-top kinds, to allow for expansion of the berries as they freeze.

PICKLING

Wild foods that can be pickled include poke shoots, milkweed flower clusters and seed pods, and purslane tips. If you want to pickle a small amount, just add it to the juice in a pickle jar after some or all of the pickles have been removed. It will be well pickled in a few weeks.

In the books *Putting Food By, Joy of Cooking,* and other cookbooks you will find many recipes for pickling.

Dried wild foods should be stored in a dark place.
These were put in a window briefly to show that you
can have wild foods in winter, too.

Glossary

ALTERNATE LEAVES—Leaves which grow singly on a stem, usually a leaf on one side, then a leaf on the other, and so on.

BACTERIA—One-celled microscopic organisms (usually classified as plants) that cannot make their own food. Some bacteria cause disease; many aid the decay of dead plants and animals.

COMPOUND LEAVES—Leaves which are made up of two or more leaflets, attached to a central leafstalk.

FORAGING—Looking or searching for supplies, especially for food.

GENUS—In the classification of living things, a genus is made up of closely related species, for example, the genus *Vitus* contains all of the different species of grapes.

HABITAT—The living place, or immediate surroundings, of an organism.

OPPOSITE LEAVES—Leaves which grow in pairs, directly opposite one another on stems.

PECTIN—A chemical compound found in ripe fruits which causes jams, jellies, marmalades, and conserves to jell. Apples, currants, plums, and cranberries are rich in pectin. Strawberries, blueberries, peaches, raspberries, and grapes are low in pectin.

PERENNIAL PLANTS—Plants which have a life span of two or more years. Annual plants live for just one growing season.

PHYTOPHOBIA—Fear of plants.

PITH—Soft tissue in the center of stems and branches of most woody plants.

POLLEN—The powdery substance produced by flowering plants which is made up of individual pollen grains containing male sex cells.

POT LIQUOR—Also called vegetable water, this is the liquid in which vegetables have been cooked. It usually contains vitamins and minerals from the vegetables and, whenever possible, should be served with them or used in other ways, such as in homemade soups.

QUICHE—A custard, usually made with cheese, which is baked in a pie shell and served warm. Pronounced *keesh*.

RHIZOME—A rootlike stem which usually grows horizontally underground and has roots on its lower surface and shoots or leaves growing from its upper surface.

ROSETTE—A circular cluster of leaves, usually at ground level. Dandelion leaves form rosettes.

SAUTÉ—To fry lightly in an open pan.

SPILE—A hollow tube, usually made of wood, through which maple sap flows, then drips into a collecting container.

TUBER—An enlarged underground stem in which food is stored (as in daylily and potato plants). Tubers commonly develop at the end of rhizomes.

Further Reading

Angier, Bradford. *Field Guide to Common Wild Edibles*. Harrisburg, Pa.: Stackpole Books, 1974. A paperback book showing good-sized color paintings of 116 edible plants, with brief text about food preparation. This is a very useful identification guide (though the knotweed illustration is of a Northern species, not the widespread Japanese knotweed).

———. *Feasting Free on Wild Edibles*. Harrisburg, Pa.: Stackpole Books, 1972. A 288-page paperback which complements Angier's field guide; the black-and-white drawings are small and not too helpful for identification, but the text includes many recipes.

Arnold, Robert, and Pearce, Laer. "Burgeoning Cult of Wild Food Nourishes Fatal Misconceptions." *Smithsonian*, May 1977, pp. 48–55. Though it reflects a "nature is dangerous" attitude, this article does have colored illustrations of several species of poisonous plants.

Berglund, Berndt, and Bolsby, Clare. *The Edible Wild*. New York: Scribner's, 1971. Treating forty edible plants in detail, this book is especially useful for those who live in northern United States and Canada (the authors are Canadians). The black-and-white drawings are big enough to be useful identification guides. For each plant there are several recipes; some are quite ambitious and call for ingredients which may not be readily available—such as moose! The book concludes with an illustrated section on some common poisonous plants. (Interestingly, poke is listed as a poisonous plant, while other foraging books stress the edibility of young poke shoots and Euell Gibbons called poke "the most widely used wild vegetable in America.")

Brackett, Babette, and Lash, Maryann. *The Wild Gourmet*. Boston: Godine Press, 1975. Available in hardcover and paperback, this book tells of foraging opportunities on a month-by-month basis. The abundant recipes are presented more simply and clearly than in many other wild-foods books. The emphasis is on northeastern and coastal foods (mussels, sea lettuce, periwinkles). Most of the brown-and-white drawings are good-sized and useful for identification.

Crockett, Lawrence J. *Wildly Successful Plants: A Handbook of North American Weeds*. New York: Macmillan, 1977. Available in hardcover and paperback, this book includes some important basic information about plant life and plant identification, and describes a hundred of the most common weeds, which include some trees, vines, poisonous plants, wildflowers, and many of the most abundant edible plants. The black-and-white drawings are full-page and useful for identification.

Gibbons, Euell. *Stalking the Wild Asparagus*, field guide edition. New York: McKay, 1962. Besides the clear and good-sized black-and-white drawings and the many recipes, this forager's "bible" includes information on growing wild foods indoors in winter, and also on catching fish, crayfish, and other such animals for meat courses. The text reflects Gibbons's enthusiasm, and is "like a walk in the country with a friend." If you are able to forage along seashores and estuaries, see the author's *Stalking the Blue-Eyed Scallop*. And for details about foraging adventures in the Southwest, along the Maine coast, near downtown San Francisco, and elsewhere, see Gibbons's *Stalking the Faraway Places*.

Gilbert, Sara. *You Are What You Eat*. New York: Macmillan, 1977. Loaded with common sense, this book contains basic information about nutrition and attitudes about food; it also makes it clear that food companies are not primarily interested in providing nutritious and tasty food.

Hall, Alan. *The Wild Food Trailguide*. New York: Holt, Rinehart and Winston, 1976. Designed for use by backpackers, this paperback is itself packed with useful information on edible plants, their identification, and uses for them. A 22-page section separates plants into food categories (for example, salads, potato substitutes, teas, jams, jellies) and tells their seasons of availability and the page of the book on which you'll find more details. Each of eighty-five plants is allotted two pages, with a black-and-white drawing and range map on one page. Twelve kinds of poisonous plants are also illustrated and described. This is not much of a recipe book, but otherwise is one of the best.

Hertsberg, Ruth, Vaughan, Beatrice, and Greene, Janet. *Putting Food By*. 2nd edition. Brattleboro, Vermont: The Stephen Greene Press, 1975. A clearly written, finely detailed guide to canning, freezing, drying and other ways of preserving all sorts of foods. Illustrated with drawings and photographs.

Hewitt, Jean. *The New York Times Natural Foods Cookbook.* New York: Quadrangle Books, 1971. A 434-page book containing hundreds of recipes based on "natural" foods; included are several recipes for such wild foods as dandelions, poke, blueberries, and strawberries.

Kingsbury, John. *Deadly Harvest: A Guide to Common Poisonous Plants.* New York: Holt, Rinehart and Winston, 1965. Details about plant poisons and the common poisonous species, wild and cultivated, in North America. Illustrated with small drawings and photographs.

Kirk, Donald. *Wild Edible Plants of the Western United States.* Healdsburg, Calif.: Naturegraph Publications, 1970. A comprehensive field guide, illustrated with black and white drawings of western and nationwide species, this book contains no recipes but does have some information about preparation and use of wild plants.

Kluger, Marilyn. *The Wild Flavor.* New York: Coward, McCann & Geoghegan, 1973. A 284-page hardcover book with a rambling text that dwells at length on over thirty edible wild plants. Most of the black-and-white drawings are helpful for identification, and there are many fine recipes.

Knutsen, Karl. *Wild Plants You Can Eat.* New York: Doubleday, 1975. This 94-page paperback treats twenty-four edible wild plants in detail, with well-organized advice when to harvest, how to harvest, and so forth) and several recipes for each species. The illustrations are all photographs, some of which are in color, but their value for identification is quite limited because of their small size.

Martin, Alexander. *Weeds.* New York: Golden Press, 1972. Part of the well-illustrated paperback Golden Nature Guide series, this book shows more than a hundred weeds in color, and their range in the United States; many of them are edible, and this book is an inexpensive identification aid.

Medsger, Oliver. *Edible Wild Plants.* New York: Macmillan, 1966. Originally published in 1939, this 323-page book is of little value for recipes but is the most complete wild-foods book. It is illustrated with black-and-white photos and with clear, helpful drawings. The text often tells about uses of wild foods by Indians and early settlers.

Nearing, Helen and Scott. *The Maple Sugar Book*. New York: Schocken Books, 1970. A detailed explanation of large-scale maple syrup and sugar making, with many practical ideas for small-scale producers and fascinating details about syrup making by Indians and early settlers.

Niethammer, Carolyn. *American Indian Food and Lore*. New York: Macmillan, 1974. An 8-by-11-inch paperback that emphasizes edible wild plants of the Southwest. The drawings are good-sized and accurate. There are 150 recipes, most of which were used by southwestern Indians.

Peterson, Lee. *A Field Guide to Edible Wild Plants of Eastern and Central North America*. Boston: Houghton Mifflin Company, 1978. An excellent identification aid, with clear black and white drawings supplemented by some color photographs. The book also includes brief information on food preparation, and the seasons and habitats of various species.

Pinkwater, Jill. *The Natural Snack Cookbook: 151 Good Things to Eat*. New York: Four Winds Press, 1975. A 258-page cookbook that includes basic and important information about nutrition and cooking. It tells how to prepare many nutritious treats in a simple step-by-step manner.

Pringle, Laurence. "Foraging for Food Provides Rewards for a Brave Palate." *Smithsonian*, September 1976, pp. 120–129. With some tips for beginning foragers, this article is mostly about the attitudes and experiences of Christopher Letts, the main foraging consultant for this book.

Rombauer, Irma S., and Becker, M. R. *Joy of Cooking*, rev. ed. New York: New American Library, 1973. This cook's "bible" contains over 4,300 recipes and a lot of practical information on foods and food preparation. A few wild foods, such as sorrel and watercress, are included.

Tampion, John. *Dangerous Plants*. New York: Universe Books, 1977. A well-illustrated guide to some of the most common poisonous plants, both wild and "tame."

Index

Asterisk (*) indicates photograph or drawing